APR 1 2 2018

WITHIN
THE CONTEXT
OF NO CONTEXT

Also by George W. S. Trow:
Bullies

George W. S. Trow

WITHIN
THE CONTEXT
OF NO CONTEXT

Atlantic Monthly Press
New York

"Within the Context of No Context" originally appeared in *The New Yorker* and was first published in book form by Little, Brown and Company, Boston, in 1981.

Published simultaneously in Canada
Printed in the United States of America

Library of Congress Cataloging-in-Publication Data

Trow, George W. S.
    Within the context of no context / George W. S. Trow.
        p. cm.
    Originally published: Boston : Little, Brown and Co., 1981
    ISBN: 978-0-87113-674-9
        1. United States—Civilization—1945– 2. Popular culture—United States.
    3. Trow, George W. S. I. Title.
    E169.12.T76 1997
    973.92—dc20   96-36582

Design by Laura Hammond Hough

Atlantic Monthly Press
an imprint of Grove/Atlantic, Inc.
841 Broadway
New York, NY 10003

Distributed by Publishers Group West

www.groveatlantic.com

11 12 13 14 15 16   10 9 8 7

For Tim Mayer

Contents

Collapsing
Dominant

My Family Tradition

"Within the Context of No Context," the essay republished now in this book, ends with the following paragraphs:

When I was very young—four years old, that is, and five—it was my habit in the late afternoon to stand at a window at the east end of the living room of my family's house, in Cos Cob, Connecticut, and wait for my father to come into my view. My father commuted on the New Haven Railroad in those days, and walked home from the station. When I spotted him, I waved. I usually saw him before he saw me, because my eyesight was much better than his. When he saw me he waved back and walked (I believe) at a faster pace until he was at our door. Once inside, he put down the bundle of newspapers he carried under his arm (my father, a newspaperman, brought home all three evening newspapers and, often, one or two of the morning papers as well), and hugged my mother. Then he took his fedora hat off his head and put it on mine.

3

It was assumed that I would have a fedora hat of my own by the time I was twelve years old. My father had had his first fedora hat at the age of nine, but he said he recognized that the circumstances of his bringing up had been different from the circumstances of mine (it was his opinion that his mother, my grandmother, had been excessively strict in the matter of dress), and he would not insist on anything inappropriate or embarrassing. He said that probably it would not be necessary for me to wear kid gloves during the day, ever. But certainly, he said, at the end of boyhood, when as a young man I would go on the New Haven Railroad to New York City, it would be necessary for me to wear a fedora hat. I have, in fact, worn a fedora hat, but ironically. Irony has seeped into the felt of any fedora hat I have ever owned—not out of any wish of mine but out of necessity. A fedora hat worn by me without the necessary protective irony would eat through my head and kill me. I was born into the upper middle class in 1943, and one of the strange turns my life has taken is this: I was taught by my parents to believe that the traditional manners of the high bourgeoisie, properly acquired, would give me a certain dignity, which would protect me from embarrassment. It has turned out that I am able to do almost anything but act according to those modes—this because I deeply believe that those modes are suffused with an embarrassment so powerful that it can kill. It turns out that while I am at home in many strange places, I am not free even to visit the territory I was expected to inhabit effortlessly. To wear a fedora, I must first torture it out of shape so that it can be cleaned of the embarrassment in it.

It seems to me that this new introduction, written sixteen years after "Within the Context of No Context" was published in the

New Yorker magazine, should take up where those paragraphs left off. In reading them now I am struck by my insistence on embarrassment as the writer's motive. I was misleading myself, or hiding something from myself. The perceptions of the young man I was then are suffused, I think, not with embarrassment but with a feeling of entitlement on the one hand and feverishness on the other.

I want to explain these two feelings—or qualities—now. First, the entitlement. The implication in the paragraphs I have just quoted is that I come from the upper middle class the way many other people come from the upper middle class. In fact, the circumstances are quite specific, and relevant to the essay. I come from a printing family, a media family, even a demographic or high-tech family, which in its social manners preserved the traditions of the upper middle class. Since it is short, and to the point, and since I had no direct contact with the man himself, I will quote a short description of the founder of our Trow clan in New York, published in a book about the history of printing*:

> John Fowler Trow was once described as "the most considerable printer New York has ever had, taking into view the magnitude of his office and the length of time it has continued." Trow was born in Andover, Massachusetts, in 1809, and served his apprenticeship with Flagg and Gould, a firm with a reputation for printing in Oriental languages. On the completion of his term, Trow went to Nashua, New Hampshire, and started a newspaper, but later gave it up, and went to New York, where, on May 1, 1833, he began business with John T. West under the firm name West & Trow. They separated in 1836, and Trow continued alone until 1840 when

---

*John Clyde Oswald, *Printing in the Americas,* 1937.

he established the printing firm of John F. Trow & Company, with Jonathan Leavitt, who also had come from Andover, Massachusetts, as his partner. Leavitt was a bookbinder by trade, and had formerly been associated with Daniel Appleton, founder of D. Appleton & Company, who was his brother-in-law. Leavitt and Trow formed a separate company under their combined names to do publishing and book-selling. Trow was always prompt to adopt new methods; he was among the first to use power presses; the power being a mule. In 1840, he added a stereotype department; in 1847 he began to publish directories, the Trow New York directories becoming in time a recognized city institution.

In 1855 he introduced the Mitchell typesetting machine and continued to use it for many years. He imported type fonts in many languages and specialized in the printing of books in foreign tongues. Soon after the Civil War, when William M. Tweed was in control of New York City affairs, Trow was one of those who stood in the path of the infamous boss and was, like those similarly situated, summarily removed. He was forced to sell his printing business to the New York Printing Company, which was owned by Tweed. After the downfall of the political ring headed by Tweed, and his conviction and imprisonment, Trow recovered his printing business. It was incorporated as the Trow Printing and Book-binding Company. John F. Trow died in August 1886. The Trow business continued until April 29, 1918, when it went into the hands of a receiver, and the plant was sold through second-hand dealers.

To this description of old man Trow, I will add one footnote. When I say I come from a *demographic* family, from a family long interested in demographics, I am thinking of Trow's *Directories*. Trow was a great counter. He had more people surveying New York City for his New York *Directory* than the Census Bureau had. Before Trow, directories were handbooks for the commercial elite. Trow included everyone who had a roof over his head. This was, of course, before the telephone book. In fact, Trow *invented* the telephone book.

I first encountered the world of printing in 1952 in New York City in the City Room of the *New York Post,* where my father worked. Children are the beneficiaries—and also the victims—of the theater of various moments, and I believe that both my feeling of entitlement and my feeling of feverishness have their root in my visit to the City Room of the *New York Post.* I was a vulnerable child, eager to have life make its mark on me; that is, I wanted badly to know which theater wanted me, and which theater was legitimate to me. As to the City Room of the *Post,* I found it unimaginably powerful, unimaginably netherworld in its implications, and I felt it belonged to me. The Composing Room especially, which directly adjoined the City Room, appealed to me. It was populated by old men, and the machines were not new; they belonged to the era of Trow. All the modern processes had not yet invaded New York daily newspaper life. The type was set on Mergenthaler Linotype machines; these machines were vats of molten lead. In the City Room I watched my father take "books" of text (four or five typewritten sheets constituted a "book") and walk them to the Composing Room. In the Composing Room, a man from a Friendly Hell sat at a dangerous machine and turned my father's text into a metal object. It was a process ancient and modern, both. Back in the City Room, I could feel a vibration in the floor. My father took me, then, to see the presses, which in their violent turning set the whole building ahum. These were rotary printing presses; the rotary printing press had made the modern daily newspaper possible; I knew that my father's guardian Ernest Trow Carter had married a Hoe, and that the Hoes had for many years made the best and most famous rotary presses.*

A year or so later my father told me a story. He told it light-heartedly, but I took it seriously. A man had come out of the Composing Room, having heard that there was a young man named Trow working at the City Desk. He said, "Is your name Trow?" And my father said yes. And the old man said, "I worked for the Trows."

Somehow, if you put these two incidents together—my visit to the still old-fashioned City Room of the *New York Post* in 1952 and the story of my father's encounter with that old printer—you

---

*Progress in mass printing during the middle of the nineteenth century can be compared to the exponential progress made in computers today. In May of 1879, the Missouri *Republican*, having installed new Hoe presses, gave an overview of this process:

> The press used in printing the Missouri *Gazette* from 1808 to 1822 was a Ramage, the first to be set up west of the Mississippi River. It was hard work for two men to print 75 copies on one side in an hour. The next press was the Stansberry patent lever with a capacity of 240 impressions per hour. It was followed by the Washington hand press, with which a good workman could print 300 sheets an hour, and in 1837 by an Adams power press with a capacity of 800 impressions per hour. Then came in succession the Hoe presses; in 1843 a single-cylinder; in 1853 a double cylinder; in 1858 a four cylinder, and in 1864 an eight-cylinder . . . and in May, 1879, these were supplanted by a new Hoe machine capable of printing, folding, pasting the backs and cutting the ends of 30,000 eight-page papers in one hour. [*Ibid.*]

Things slowed down after the 1920s, and the *New York Post* of 1952 would have been understandable to a man who understood the Missouri *Republican* of 1879.

have the story of my life. On the one hand, being taken very early into adult circumstances precisely so that I should acquire a feeling of entitlement and continuity, all that on the one hand, and, on the other, the feeling that my family tradition, and the traditions to which it was allied, were hanging by a very thin thread.

Don't Let Me Get Grand with You

There are just five generations of Trows in the story above, including The Old Man John Fowler Trow, whose first power press worked with the power of a mule, and myself; and I can show you that in every year from 1833 to date there has been a Trow in New York City with an interest in printing—or journalism; also, advertising and the marketing end of demography. But don't let me get grand with you. It is not an Unbroken Family Tradition. I realize now that I am a man from a broken tradition who was convinced by the theater of a moment that his tradition was unbroken and that he was the heir to it. Working as though from an unbroken tradition I have made sense of my life by developing an ability to analyze Mainstream American Cultural Artifacts, and this I also urge my fellow citizens to do.

The Fate of the Mainstream

In preparing this new introduction to "Within the Context of No Context," I consulted a few people—people who knew what I knew, but differently. I took Phyllis Cerf Wagner to lunch at the Palace Hotel. The Palace Hotel, in the old Villard Houses, used to be—I mean the old part—the headquarters of the Roman Catholic Archdiocese of New York. In the 1950s and 1960s, Random House had its headquarters across the courtyard in the northern wing of the

Villard Compound, and there I used to visit—and sometimes work with—Phyllis Wagner (then Phyllis Cerf), high in the eaves of the old mansion.

I wanted to ask Mrs. Wagner something, but I wasn't sure what. I had long known her and her family—her two sons had been close friends at Harvard. What I wanted to ask, I think, was, "What was it, exactly, that our group was doing?" But I didn't know how to ask that question so I talked about George Washington because I was then thinking about—and writing about—George Washington. "You know, I don't think that most people understand that George Washington invented the American Mainstream," I said. Mrs. Wagner looked up, interested. "You know what you've just said, don't you," she said. I did. The magic word—always had been, always would be—was "mainstream." My question—unasked—had been answered. What we had been doing was: floating in, and sometimes influencing, the mainstream. Period.

Lindy's, 1963

Men and women like Bennett Cerf and Phyllis Cerf—and my father at the *New York Post*—were people with a sense of American history, and the history of the American Mainstream of the 1920s and 1930s and 1940s, who also participated in the daily work of establishing the commercial reality of the 1950s, and the 1960s up to 1966, let's say.

I can remember once going with the Cerf family to Lindy's in the early 1960s. Lindy's was if not on its way out, past its prime. But we were still in the 1950s in a way. And an author, then well known and a best-selling author, named John Gunther, came up to the table, and what he did I have seen done many times since: he was approaching someone who controlled the construct of the moment to sell an idea. It was a Mainstream Moment; so it is a

Mainstream Moment now, in 1996, when someone approaches Quentin Tarentino to sell an idea. The process is the same; the moments are very different. In Lindy's in 1963, one could still assume that some World War II seriousness was at work in the popular market. One does not—cannot—make that assumption now. John Gunther was going to write *Inside Latin America Again*, or *Behind the Iron Curtain, Now*, or something like that. But even then, Lindy's, 1963, we all sensed that it was cracking.

La Dolce Vita

There were a few of us in my generation, then, who, in the 1970s, were socially active because we were equipped for it, and because it was our inheritance, who had a sense memory of the social construct of the 1950s (and back of that the 1920s, 1930s, and 1940s). I mean, the sons of Phyllis and Bennet Cerf; the son and daughter of Russell Crouse (*Life with Father* to *The Sound of Music*); the son of Arlene Francis and Martin Gabel; the son of Moss Hart and Kitty Carlisle Hart; all these people—and they were my friends—were *generationally* poised to participate in the social life of New York during the 1970s. The parents of my friends were far more important than my father was in the social construct of the 1950s, on the one hand; on the other hand, my mind was always going back to the nineteenth century. Timothy Crouse's father had adapted *Life with Father* for the stage; but I was living within the construct of *Life with Father*. My friends knew that almost all situation comedies were in some relation to the groundbreaking work of George S. Kauffman and Moss Hart (*You Can't Take It With You* is the template for *Full House, Friends, Boston Common*, and just about 5,000 more of them); on the other hand I knew that the men and women who had created the Modern Commercial Mainstream in the 1920s and 1930s had been in relation to the city of the 1880s and 1890s

(Back of *that,* thank God, I did not go. Edmund Wilson or Robert Lowell I am not; the Civil War is a closed book to me.) In any case, the group of twenty- and thirty-year-olds I am discussing, geared from birth to go out in the life of New York City in young adulthood, *did* go out in the life of the city in the 1970s, and what we saw was—Fellini. Earl Wilson was a gossip columnist for the *New York Post.* "That's Earl, Brother!" was his sign-off; his jokes were called "Earl's Pearls"; his nightclub chatter was called "The Midnight Earl"; I saw Earl Wilson in the 1970s totter from half-empty nightclub to half-empty nightclub. To say that he was an object of terror for me was putting it mildly because, knowing the process, I knew he would inevitably come back.

Remember
Remember, in the situation I am describing *the referee always wins.*

Collapsing Dominant
Each one of these social generations—from the '50s, from the '60s, from the '70s, from the Reagan era, from now—thinks of its social aesthetic as definitive. In fact, they are all in a process: encouraged toward, and beyond, hubris, by demography.

Sweet Smell of Success
Everyone knows, or ought to know, that there has happened under us a Tectonic Plate Shift, or over us a Cosmic Tick-Tock. In any case, the buildings are the same: this one a sweet Victorian cottage, that one an old brick tenement out of Hopper; there, on the hill, is yet another new Tara, all columns and Cadillacs; the political parties

have the same names; we still have a CBS, an NBC, and a *New York Times;* but we are not the same nation that had these things before.

And, suddenly, we want them all so badly. We have magazines to support our love for the Victorian. We all want a real network. The New American, once again all optimism and make-it-work, hungers for exactly what drove an earlier generation to distraction, almost to madness. *Sweet Smell of Success,* a film of 1957, a film made by a brilliant director named Alexander Mackendrick, chronicles exactly the unattractive (to me) dominance system of the 1950s. Men and women under thirty-five, I happen to know, watch this film with wonder and awe: how can we get a piece of that, they ask themselves, and one another.

In April of 1957, my father took me to a gathering at the Yale Club of boys from the New York area who were to attend Exeter, my father's school, in the fall. This happened, and that happened, but what happened in my deepest self, which is aesthetic, was that I met a boy like myself. His name was Robert Ferdinand Wagner III, and he was the son of the mayor of New York City. Three years ago I attended a memorial service for this friend at St. Patrick's Cathedral in New York. Between the city portrayed in *Sweet Smell of Success* in 1957 and the strange dispirited memorial service for Bobby Wagner in 1994, where the remnants of liberal New York stood or sat stunned, wondering what could have happened to them—between these two events is the New York City of my direct experience.

"Giuliani was expecting Bobby to tell him what to do," a friend told me after the service. My mind went back to 1957. Bobby knew a lot *then.* He was brilliant, and his father, the mayor, took him completely into his confidence. Presiding over the world portrayed in *Sweet Smell of Success* was Mayor Wagner, and ever at his side, enthralled, listening to every word, giving him a kiss on meeting and at parting, was Bobby. Getting all the good information, and living gently.

The anthropology of our situation—I mean mine and Bobby's—in 1957 was quite complicated. Two phrases in use at the time were: "The Military-Industrial Complex" and "Ivy League." That is a good place to start. Well, we don't have those things anymore, and both were concrescences, things formed out of many other things, like the media conglomerates being formed now. My immediate sympathy with Bobby Wagner, I now think, had to do with a sense that we had both been handed, in slightly different ways, the same impossible task: to love the unlovable; to love *Sweet Smell of Success* and send it both back and forward—back into a happier American history and forward into a fairer future. The world of *Sweet Smell of Success* was of course just the result of human struggle within the context of something like despair.

Movies are always attractive. If a woman gets her face slapped in a movie, the woman is attractive, and the slap has the force of shock. I see things on the street every day that have never been shown in a movie: hopelessness in human eyes; the real dead end. The script for *Sweet Smell of Success* is very good; it is by Clifford Odets and Ernest Lehman, but it is pale next to the writing of Nathanael West in his account of daily journalism in *Miss Lonelyhearts*. His villain Shrike has none of J. J. Hunsecker's animal magnetism, and could not be played by Burt Lancaster, as Odets' Hunsecker was. Early in *Miss Lonelyhearts* Shrike and Miss Lonelyhearts meet in a speakeasy. "If you need a synthesis, here is the kind of material to use," Shrike says, and West writes:

He took a clipping from his wallet and slapped it on the bar.

ADDING MACHINE USED IN RITUAL OF WESTERN SECT . . . Figures Will Be Used for Prayers for Condemned Slayer of Aged Recluse . . . Denver, Colo., Feb. 2 (A.P.). Frank H. Rice, Supreme Pontiff of the Liberal Church of America, has announced he will carry out his plan for a "goat and adding machine" ritual for William Moya, condemned slayer, despite objection to his program by a Cardinal of the sect. Rice declared the goat would be used as part of a "sack cloth and ashes" service shortly before and after Moya's execution, set for the week of June 20. Prayers for the condemned man's soul will be offered on an adding machine. Numbers, he explained, constitute the only universal language. Moya killed Joseph Zemp, an aged recluse, in an argument over a small amount of money.

Miss Lonelyhearts was first published in 1933 and reflects the world of journalism of the 1920s. I have quoted the passage above because by use of it I can explain Sweet Smell of Success, and my life, to myself, and why Bobby Wagner died young. West's "'goat and adding machine' ritual" story was relevant to the world of the 1920s, and it is relevant to the world we live in now. It was not overtly relevant to the world of Sweet Smell of Success. New York in 1957 was the New York of Rodgers and Hammerstein in the country of Eisenhower, the Military-Industrial Complex, and the "Ivy League" style. We were war winners and we had Responsibilities. But the world of the "'goat and adding machine' ritual" was pulsating under all these things, and this Mackendrick's movie shows: the goat and the adding machine moving through the thin surface of civility we had built for ourselves. When I say that this "goat and adding machine" clipping explains my life to myself I mean that I always knew that the goat and the adding machine were running the show; that the goat and the adding machine were embedded in the mind that created the text of daily journalism and would out. To put it another way, I always knew that the New America had been created forever in the 1920s.

Sweet Smell of Success was not a very successful movie when it was released, and despite its air of classic restraint and its literary merit, *Miss Lonelyhearts* was viewed with suspicion during the 1950s. It was Bohemian. It was read by Bohemian boys at Exeter. Boys who read *On the Road* also, perhaps, had read *Miss Lonelyhearts* and *The Day of the Locust* by West. There was a red vinyl record, "A Coney Island of the Mind," by Lawrence Ferlinghetti; Ginsberg's "Howl" and a paperback edition of a compilation entitled *Existentialism from Dostoyevsky to Sartre*, by the American editor of Nietzsche. These items defined the style of Bohemian boys at Exeter in the late 1950s. The official style of Exeter in the late '50s was in two parts: respect for ancient rituals (shorn of their mystical or religious significance), on the one hand, and belief in the power of Modern Academic Vectors, on the other. We Bohemian boys knew that this was a system programmed to fail; we were ritual- and truth-hungry. In the phrase "respect for ancient rituals," the accent fell, at Exeter in those days (the last days in which a Patriarchy was going to be discussed or planned for), on the word "respect." A lighter accent fell on "ancient," and the word "rituals" was barely whispered. The fact that all of the ancient wisdoms we were being taught to respect had evolved out of and were dependent on rituals was—ignored. The ritual part was to be supplied, perhaps, by our belief in Academic Vectors. We Bohemian boys had no belief in Academic Vectors. I know why I had no belief in them; I knew there was a Goat and Adding Machine Ritual out there working a mile a minute, and that it was more powerful than anything in its path. It was working in my own family; it was the ritual of Daily Journalism.

I think I was trying to raise a hue and cry when I wrote "Within the Context of No Context" early in 1980, but at the time I wasn't sure just what hue and cry I was raising. I could express only a kind of informed confusion. "I have seen your best experiments and they don't work." Kind of John Reed in reverse. Now, from the distance of sixteen years, I think I was saying, "THE TWENTIES ARE COMING, THE TWENTIES ARE COMING." I think I was right; the 1920s were in the wings, then.

There were a group of boys at Exeter in the mid- and late 1950s who were called (and called themselves) "negos." They were boys with a "negative attitude." It was a group defined by a mood; it was not a clique. There were negos who were also Bohemian, but there were also nego athletes, and there were negos at the top of the honor roll. I was a Bohemian, in the sense of having read Ginsberg, Kerouac, and West (and because I took a copy of *Existentialism from Dostoyevsky to Sartre* with me wherever I went for almost a year), and I was a nego. I followed the line of the Negative Attitude through the 1960s and 1970s. It was one of the threads of continuity I held onto in an era in which continuity was being lost forever. The 1960s weren't the 1920s again; they were the Liberal Arts expressed in the negative. The 1970s, despite the hedonism, weren't the 1920s; they were the Negative out to get all the rewards formerly held by the Positive. The Goat and Adding Machine Ritual is now.

Thank You, Roman Polanski

A certain cynicism: I am writing this in Alaska. Yesterday, I conversed with a man of the kind most Americans are afraid of now. The man began the conversation defiantly: was I, or was I not, the kind of man who would talk honestly about the corruption in our country. This man would not have understood the phrase "Weimar Republic," but I understood that he was testing me; he knew that things were rotten—did I? We locked eyes. Since I am a stranger here, I let him lead. What was it I was doing in Alaska, he wanted to know. I said that I had come looking for a very quiet place in order to write a film script. That interested him, but not from the point of view of fandom. He watched a lot of movies, he said. Was I aware that movies were all done from a political motive? Had I seen *The Net*? Did I understand that they—the government, some-one—was trying to establish mistrust of free speech on the Internet? He described the movie *The Net*. Apparently, in that movie, some-one stalks someone over the Internet. That is what my interlocu-tor said, anyway. I haven't seen the movie. I paused. I didn't know quite what to say. Then I thought, maybe this man just doesn't know about ordinary cynicism, so I described the process by which most films get made. "You see," I said, "most people are just trying to make money; you have to grab the attention of people fast, the audience, finally, but first the moneyman or film executive you are pitching the film to. Film executives aren't all that intelligent, so you make sure that your idea has something identified with the new right up front, but then very quickly, you relate that new thing to something the film executive already knows and identifies with Complete Utter Safe Success. For instance," I said, "the person who wanted to make the movie *The Net* might simply have said to his boss that he wanted to make *Fatal Attraction* on the Internet." My interlocutor was interested, and began to trust me.

Leaving this man, I thought about a father and a son, now both dead. The son was my best friend and my partner. His father sur-vived him, and one night, one difficult night, I found myself having dinner alone with him. This man—the father of my friend—was, let us call him, a businessman. He had lived in the world of *Miss Lonely-hearts* but wasn't going to let it get him down. He was a brilliant man, but he had had to go to a hardscrabble law school, while people less brilliant got to go to fine and pretty places. He sent his son to fine and pretty places, all the time making sure that his son knew the contempt he felt in his heart (he said it was contempt) for the fine and the pretty. Years before, I had seen this man in his office in Boston (he was the head of and the proprietor of a Sporting Goods Conglomerate). Over his shoulder, as I entered his office, I could see the Boston Public Library—that nice building by McKim, Mead and White. I said something about the library, how nice it was to have that view from one's office. Mr. X turned slowly around and looked at the library, as though for the first time. "Oh, is that the public library?" he said. "I didn't know." He said all this with contempt. References to the fine and pretty from the fine and pretty he didn't need, was his point of view. I fell into silence, which was what he wanted. He wanted me to shut my mouth, and he knew how to get that.

He was of course a little bit more mellow with me after his son died. He was, mostly, I think, sentimental about himself. He was alone in life, now, and so forth. I knew how to play him. I flattered. I asked about his business career. I was a cold-hearted detective. What was this man's story, I wondered. How was it that he had survived his son, the son being so much stronger of mind and heart. I asked if he had had a mentor, anyone to tell him, you know, useful things to carry into life. He laughed. It was the only real laugh I ever heard him let out. He told me about a man from upstate New York who had been a sharp salesman. "He was the sharpest man I ever met," Mr. X said. "We went out to dinner one night, kind of like this"—and here Mr. X gave me something like a sympathetic "you're all right, kid" nod as I sat opposite him at the dinner table at a big vulgar expensive restaurant—"and he told me, 'Jerry, the American people are interested in only two things: astrology, and their bowels.' I never forgot that."

Nor will I ever forget it. It's the Secret of America. For seventy years America has been constructed and deconstructed from that point of view.

So, Americans are, let us call it, self-absorbed on the one hand or masturbatory, and the cynical processes that address these "qualities" do tend to eat through civility. In this situation, conversation becomes difficult. There is more under the table, so to speak, than on the table. Mr. X had been, during the years during which our Military-Industrial Complex was built, one of two men who "really ran" (Mr. X's phrase) the General Instrument Company. Then, after the war, he bought a small sporting goods company and "romanced it" (his phrase) into the Conglomerate. (Then it went bust—the Romance went sour, I guess—but Mr. X had by that time separated his own finances from the Romance, so it was more Hard Cheese on someone else, not him.) But all that time he had been operating from the principle that Americans were interested in just two things—astrology and their bowels. He had been to law school, but the law was just a means of regulating a generality that reacted to astrology and their bowels; he had sold people fishing rods and Oriental Electronics (his Conglomerate was one of the first to get into Oriental Electronics), but all the time he was thinking about Daily Evacuation and the Stars.

Thank You, Roman Polanski II

My interlocutor in Alaska has, by my perception, no sense of the Sequence of What Has Been Possible in the movie business. For instance, he doesn't know (by my perception) that there wasn't much in the way of the Demonic in Mainstream films before *Rosemary's Baby*, by Roman Polanski. Mr. Polanksi had a sense, I guess, that there was more going on under the table of our fine and pretty American life than there was on. I can remember when *Rosemary's Baby* was in release. The marketing people for the movie (just ordinary American businesspeople, now, almost certainly, in Graceful Retirement in Hilton Head or Sun City) had the chance, thanks to Roman Polanski, to exercise something like full freedom in relation to their perception that Americans were interested most of all in astrology and their bowels. It must have been a heady moment. Contact with one's animus, in a way. Truth at last, in a way. In any case, they had arranged for the little motto of the film ("Pray for Rosemary's Baby") to be stenciled on the pavement of New York City streets, at crosswalks. You would be walking down Fifth Avenue, say; you would look into the windows at Saks, say; and then you would move down the street. You would stop for a red light. The light turned green; you looked down to be sure of your footing, and there you would see—echo of Thomas Pynchon's end-of-the-world book *The Crying of Lot 49*—a little secret message to one's secret self. "Pray for Rosemary's Baby." I never saw the movie, but I knew it was a hit.

Thank You, Roman Polanski III

People need to understand (as they say now) that nothing that doesn't appeal immediately to ten million people happens in the serious mass-media business; ten million people immediately, fifty in potential. That puts a lot of things out of the running. A new delicate insight into the works of Thomas Hardy—hard work to put across. What you need is something people are in denial about that they want to see you take the risk of expressing. I am talking now from the screenwriter's point of view. Imagine yourself a fatherless family: you don't have a father who patiently takes you through those rites of passage he knows to be necessary (and which he knows how to navigate). Rather, you have a congeries of crazy aunts and uncles who appear from time to time, shouting at the top of their lungs about something they know you are in denial about; mostly what you are in denial about is your sense of having been abandoned.

Thank You, Roman Polanski IV

Roman Polanski seems to have had the insight that our thin layer of civility in America was a membrane as thin as the talk at a supermarket, and that everything was going on somewhere else with us. Hitchcock had this insight, too, but worked it another way. Hitchcock was Aeschylus to Polanski's Sex Pistols as to American Horror. I had a friend named Michael O'Donoghue, for many years the head writer at *Saturday Night Live*, who was very tolerant about anarchic expression. He was opposed to Redeeming Social Value, or so he said. For cultural avatars beyond his pale, he had an expression: "I wouldn't touch that with Roman Polanski," he used to say.

Abandoned

Democracy opens up the possibility of "abandonment," and creates opportunities for men and women who understand how to play to or on that feeling.

Good-bye, John Marquand

In 1958, in the era of *Sweet Smell of Success* and six months after I entered Exeter, my family moved to Bedford, New York. In Cos Cob we had lived in a middle-class house in a middle-class neighborhood. In Bedford, we lived in a middle-class house in an upper-class neighborhood. The change was profound. Here were people who had authority within the Military-Industrial Complex, who kept to older rituals. Their rituals, one almost wants to say, were agricultural. They had their dogs; they had their horses; on the face of it they seemed to have been defined by their dogs and horses. In

America (the land of no nuance, as to popular entertainment; the land of the very broad stroke) small changes in real social reality can be logarithmic. Four baby steps in a certain direction and you are in Oz instead of Kansas. I am not thinking only of my own history, here. In 1958, the people I had moved next door to not only were universally considered to make up the ruling group of the country; they owned the rituals: the schools, the clubs, the ladders. Part of their style was to say, "But of course we're just ordinary Americans." Five years later they *were* just ordinary Americans, and their rituals—including the dogs and the horses, maybe—were burdens, and were so perceived by their children.

These people had their own literature. To some extent their moral dilemmas were of interest to the country at large. A part of the reading and film-going public wanted good—or better—information about their secret rulers, just as, at a later date, part of the public would want an honest account of the life and death of John Lennon. Behind the scenes isn't always a bad idea for a book, if the actors really are powerful, and if their moral dilemmas are real and placed correctly in context—and in sequence. My new neighbors had had their stories told—or indicated—by John O'Hara and by John Marquand. *From the Terrace* is the last important book to talk to—or about—the group I am discussing. One wouldn't mention it, except that a huge part of our population seems to be scrambling back to the Terrace—a terrace that has been swept clean, however, of moral dilemmas. *Point of No Return*, by John Marquand, would seem to me to be the important book in the postwar O'Hara-Marquand oeuvre. It tells the story of a man from the milieu I am describing whose values are in conflict. He has taken his liberal arts education (the one owned by the upper class) seriously; on the other hand, he is in competition for high office at his bank.

Which way will he go? The story is poignant from the point of view of this moment. No one who showed the mildest suggestion of the kind of conflictedness Marquand's hero was feeling could get in the door of his bank now. I want to return to the sequence and context of my life now. When I entered Exeter in 1957, what I saw was the O'Hara-Marquand world dissolving. "You've got to be kidding" was the point of view of the "negos" of the school, and the negos were the really bright boys. This atmosphere presented a strange difficulty for me. By my perception, the negos, my group, were in reaction to *Sweet Smell of Success*. That kind of effectiveness within anarchy (with a little jazz in it) was just what they liked. They liked lingo (we had our own private language); and they liked to be mean—real mean. Naturally, I understood what was going on—I had been raised in it. At the same time, when my father put his arm around my shoulder and took me to the Yale Club in the spring of 1957 he was saying to me, "Now you'll get into the real thing," by which he meant the set of moral concerns Marquand's hero in *Point of No Return* had turned away from, circa 1949. The atmosphere at Exeter in 1957–59 was, I know, strange for many boys there—especially the sons of fathers who had powerfully demonstrated an interest in the Liberal Arts Mainstream; I am thinking now of the sons of John Hersey, Arthur Schlesinger, Jr., John Galbraith, and of my friend Timothy Marquand, John Marquand's son. But I think it was strangest of all for Bobby Wagner—and me. We were under strict instruction to find the fine and pretty within our tradition and stick to it. In very different ways our fathers had said to us, "What I do to maintain a position within the nonce construct of New York City is—just that; what I do. But I am always thinking about—Roosevelt. Go and find him for me and bring him home."

Collapsing Dominant

I am especially proud of one or two sections of "Within the Context of No Context," the essay for which this essay is an introduction. I think the central formulation was correct: that it was the role of television to establish the context of no-context, and then chronicle it. And I think that's happened. This period may, however, be at an end. The formulation that interests me most, in rereading the essay, is something only hinted at: I suggested, in 1980, that the two grids of American life—the grid of intimacy, of one person alone, and the grid of two hundred million—I suggested that these two grids had moved so far apart that something would necessarily appear in the middle distance. This was a formulation I was then struggling toward, or with. I can remember that what I had specifically in mind was something called EST, the Erhard Seminars Training, something put forward by a man named Werner Erhard, something very popular for a while in the '70s. I was taken by my friend Stephen Paley in Los Angeles to see not Mr. Erhard himself—or it may have been Mr. Erhard. In any case, it was a group of privileged Angelenos who were there to get some spiritual stuff mixed with some authority. And it was the authority component that was new. There was some interesting confusion about Mr. Erhard himself—he seemed to have a German name, but he had, perhaps, a Jewish identity; there was some interest in that, and also in the fact that the Erhard Seminars Training called for some sacrifice in terms of personal freedom. EST was famous at the time for not allowing you to go to the bathroom during a certain period of the training. This seems utterly absurd as I write this now, but it hit a spirit of the moment, a mid-1970s moment; people had, for four or five—or for some people ten—years, brooked no authority whatsoever on any subject, and this man, Erhard, realized that the time had come to insert within the realm of total permission—because the point of the Erhard Seminars Training was to open up even more options, even more freedom, even more everything—some little bit of discipline. It was debated whether it was a good thing or a bad that he wouldn't let you leave the room during a certain time frame to go to the bathroom. In any case, with some curiosity I went to this event and—there was another rule enforced in this introduction to EST. You had to wear a name tag, and the name tag couldn't include your last name. Authority just from the other point of view, you see. The overturning of anything you would have thought of as being old authority, because, of course, your last name is your old-authority point of identification—the obliteration of old authority linked to this tiny point of new authority, of not being allowed to go to the bathroom.

That was the established theater of what was going on; and within that established theater were all of these infinite promises of infinite everything—regardless of who you were; regardless of what your name was or what your family history had been, or your schooling had been, or your class had been; if you allowed your past to be obliterated, and you accepted this piece of discipline about not going to the bathroom, everything was going to be given yet a new way. And, of course, the people he was addressing were people to whom everything already had been given. And, in effect, Erhard was satisfying a relentless acquisitiveness on the part of these people. These people were powerful, many of them, in the construct of the '70s; they brooked no opposition; they had no prosperity problems; but, really, all they could think of was to make their opportunities even more grandiose, and they instinctively understood that the way to do that was to obliterate their last name and accept arbitrary discipline. Well, this interested and depressed me, and I didn't like it. I liked my last name. So, because I am a shrewd person, a foxy person sometimes, and because I'd been at cocktail parties, and for lots of other reasons, I obeyed the instruction, but—lied. I said my name was Sam, or Bill. And then I asked a question—a noncombative question, just a simple informational question, to see how it was, what it felt like, to be stroked or disciplined when you'd given a wrong name. And it was tonic. That is, the man used my spurious first name every other word. He said, "Now, Sam, the reason, Sam, you've asked that question, Sam, is that you're voicing very legitimate doubts, Sam; but, Sam, look around you: there are Joan, and Bob and Bill, and, Sam, we're here . . ." And it went on and on and on, and I said to myself, I never have to do this again.

When I wrote "Within the Context of No Context," I had in mind that EST seminar, as a prime example of the kind of strange reaction—to authority and to options—that I saw rising among my own generation and the generation immediately younger than mine. But some instinct told me that EST-like phenomena were not going to be definitive. And so I didn't write in the essay the story I've just recounted, because I felt that couldn't last, and I had no idea of what would come after.

As I say, I think the period for which the formulation I enunciated in "Within the Context of No Context"—that television would establish the context of no-context and chronicle it—I think the period for which that formulation was valid is now coming to an end. I think the O. J. Simpson trial helped. I think what is coming now is, or will be, a rejection of the 1970s as subtext for American social life. I think this rejection will come in several ways, from several quadrants, all destined to be in conflict. This will happen for the simple reason that no one who looks at it can possibly accept *Animal House* or the Erhard Training Seminars as a basis from which to live. I've spotted two trends—one within the media, and one on what we will call the Ground. There is to be a new cable television channel called TVLand. And on TVLand one will view, as entertainment, Classic Commercials. The announcement I saw included a shot of a commercial with Barbara Feldon for Top Brass hair preparation for men. She looked a little Courrèges in the picture I saw; of another time, suddenly. I put this together with the vogue for Jackie Onassis when young, for Grace Kelly when young, for Audrey Hepburn when young. I think people will reinvent their history using specific images from a more organized moment. On the ground, but operating from the same motive—a refusal to accept the 1970s subtext as a basis for continuing in American social life—we have groups like the Freemen. I think the Freemen in their essential energy go back to the Whiskey Rebellion. George Washington put down the Whiskey Rebellion two ways: he gathered an army bigger than the army he fought the British with, and he invoked his own personal authority, a personal authority greater than that possessed by any man then alive. We don't have that man today.

Media Culture is confusing in several different ways. Actually, it is confusing in one way I remember quite well—from Exeter. As I say, at Exeter in those days, we were ritual- and truth-hungry. Great Events, Great Writers, Great Men and Women, Great Wisdom Systems were all on the table at once, sans ritual. Here you had Socrates, there you had Beethoven, and who could tell the one from the other. They all belonged to a club—the Club of Those Who Had Gone Before. Was the Epicurean Life something George Eliot embraced, or was she more of a Hegel girl? And if she had never heard of Hegel, what did that mean? And if there were more people on the face of the earth who understood Nietzsche in 1957 than there had been in 1890, what did that mean in the face of television—or rock and roll? It was all too much for us then in the book department, and now it is all too much for almost everyone in the media department. So much for easy ways out. Once again, people are ritual- and truth-hungry. Once again, they have no sense of the sequence in which the cultural objects they are in reference to took their shape. I am thinking of my conversation with the prerevolutionary man in Alaska. I could show him, I know, the movie version of *From the Terrace*, the one with Paul Newman, and I bet his reaction to it would be mild—just *Dallas* another way; a tame *Dallas*. Then I could play him "The Times They Are A-Changin'," by Bob Dylan, and maybe he already knows it—or could hum it. Then I could sit down with him and watch an episode of *Beverly Hills, 90210*—one of the episodes with the boy who looks more than a little like James Dean. I don't believe he would see conspiracy in any of these artifacts. He just doesn't happen to know that he is seeing first an artifact from the Age of Our American Metternich (Dwight Eisenhower presided over an essentially reactionary World Concert, after all), then an artifact from the career of our American—I mean born in America—Tom Paine, and then an artifact from the Age of '70s Subtext—EST, *Animal House*, and Anything You Want, Configured Any Way You Want It; he just wouldn't know that he was seeing a war, Dominant Collapsing into Dominant. There weren't many boys who got taken into *Sweet Smell of Success* early enough to understand the 1970s from a 1950s control group point of view. I was one, Bobby Wagner another; a third was Warren Lyons, the son of the gossip columnist Leonard Lyons. I used to run into Warren from time to time during the 1970s. Once, at a nightclub called Reno Sweeney, we watched an entertainer named Genevieve Waite. This was just a few years after the Fillmore East had closed. Maybe Warren and I had thought the Fillmore, and all it represented, was going to be definitive for our generation, and here we were in a nightclub. Genevieve Waite had just sung a song called "Romance Is on the Rise."

"Romance is coming back, Warren," I said.

"You know what's coming back?" Warren said. "Everything; then it's going away for good."

The Road to Ritalin

Warren Lyons and I, at a nightclub twenty-five years ago, like the "negos" at Exeter in 1957, like Quentin Tarantino now, were reacting to *much too much information* absent a reliable ritual for healthy masculine development. I read in the newspaper not long ago that between 10 and 12 percent of American male children between the ages of six and fourteen are on Ritalin. It calms them down; it clams them up; it makes them controllable; it overcomes some of the *symptoms*, at least, of Attention Deficit Syndrome. It must be annoying—or maddening—to these naturally active, curious, aggressive young males to understand intuitively (as they surely must do—looking at *Animal House*, say, or *Natural Born Killers*, say, or *Pulp Fiction*, say) that they are being drugged out of the mind-set of the culture they are in natural reaction to.

I have described Exeter as it was in 1957. I was thirteen in 1957. I was on the road to Ritalin then, and so were many of the brightest boys at the school. What was the mind-set of the culture I was in natural reaction to? It was the mind-set of *Sweet Smell of Success, pretending* that the *Point of No Return* hadn't been crossed. I was already in the *Sweet Smell of Success* (aroma therapy, in a way), but I was being asked to pretend that the moral dilemmas of a Marquand Hero were alive and kicking, which they were not.

What of an American male child *born* in 1957? What would have been the cultural mind-set he met at the age of thirteen—in 1970? Papa's on pot, and Mama's gearing up for EST. *No* information about the Goat and Adding Machine Ritual (all that's been defeated forever; never mind that both Papa and Mama are deeply *into* the world of pleasure and celebrity) and no memory that the moral dilemmas of a Marquand Hero existed *ever*.

And an American male child born in 1970? Looking deeply around him in 1983? All social memory has been completely obliterated. Back to the Terrace—any way you can get there (I mean John O'Hara's DuPont, North Shore of Long Island Terrace)—with a tantalizing sense of a moment (sometime around the moment of his birth), when the Old Terrace was *destroyed* at the biggest, most drop-dead party ever held in the history of the human race.

And an American male child born in 1983? Turning thirteen as I write this? Well, if he's bright, aggressive, curious, and in natural reaction to the cultural facts outlined above, there is a 10 percent or a 12 percent chance that he's been drugged. But what are the chances that he is "hyperactive" in some new way that has never been in any doctor's office? The Road to Ritalin is, of course, a *prosperous* road. Your classroom is of a kind that *can* be disrupted; your family life is of a kind where "acting out" is noticed; where a "solution" is called for—and implemented. What of those young aggressive hyperactive males who live in perfect harmony with their surround; whose hyperactivity is in perfect harmony with some new form of criminal life taking shape now? What *is* the overall statistic on these New Males? Ten percent? Twelve percent? Twenty percent? One in ten? One in five? One in *three*?

See Ya; Don't Want to Be Ya

In 1968 I drove with a young black friend to his hometown of Docena, Alabama. We drove south in my Barracuda convertible. The songs we listened to on the car radio were "The Fool on the Hill" (my friend sang along; his voice was very good), "Grazin' in the Grass" ("What a gas!"); also "Harper Valley P.T.A." and "Ode to Billie Jo" ("The day Billie Jo McAllister jumped off the Tallahachee bridge").

I found a welcome in Docena. Immediately, I made friends with my friend's youngest brother, Matthew, who was six at the time. I could say that Matthew went with me everywhere I went (certainly we were nearly always together), but in fact, I followed him; it was his hometown after all. We had fun, putting it mildly.

Three years ago I was in the South, and I said to myself, "I must call the Hannahs in Docena." I did. When I drove in (in a rented car this time), Matthew was standing on the porch of his mother's house—six foot four with a wife and four children of his own. It was fun, putting it mildly. I invited Matthew and his wife to visit me in New York State, and they came. Matthew and I talked about Docena, and I asked him about the drug problem there. "Oh, we got one," Matthew said. "When did it start?" I asked. Matthew, without a moment's hesitation, gave me a specific date—in the middle '80s, as I remember. Like "July 16, 1985." I believe he could have given me the *hour*. That is, at a certain moment, in a certain year, not so very long ago, a certain individual came to this small, unto-itself place outside Birmingham, Alabama, and changed the history of the community. Matthew told me a little of the *mores* and *lingo* of the drug dealers who have serviced Docena. They have (wonder of wonders!) found their way into the *Sweet Smell of Success*. (Aroma therapy.) In their own mind they are in the vestibule of "21" in New York, about to get closer to the *baddest, meanest* man in America—whoever that mysterious person is, with a telephone sitting next to him at and on Table Number One. "I know; that wonder boy of yours opens next week at the Latin Quarter. Say good-bye, Lester." That marvelous freedom to operate with complete contempt—and command everyone's "respect" at the same time—*from Table Number One*.

The drug dealers who service Docena have a saying. They say it to their customers after the exchange of drugs for money has been made. It is "See ya; don't want to be ya."

Something in Common

It may interest the young African-American male to know that he really *has* something in common with his white counterpart. Think of my dead partner's father, the man who "really ran" the General Instrument Company, who had his own sporting goods conglomerate, and who had for a son one of the most talented men America has ever produced. *His* philosophy, inherited from some *shrewd old bastard* from Upper New York State (someone who really knew what was what; over whose eyes no one ever pulled the wool), his philosophy was, reduced to its essentials, "See ya, don't want to be ya." There, *there* we have our multicultural *common ground*.

Wisdom from a Child

Matthew has a young son, Erik. Erik is one of those children whose nature it is to take adult responsibility. One day, Matthew told me, Erik came to him and said, "Daddy, there isn't enough food in the ice box."

"Tell your mother," Matthew told Erik.

No, Daddy. It's *your* job to buy and fry," Erik said.

Many Ways to Look at It

Well, of course it's not *all* going away for good. But something *has* gone away for good. As I say, I come from a family which, over a long time, has been interested in demography, so let me take you

back to Lindy's in 1963, and see if I can show you what was going
away for good *then*.

World War II changed the demography. For a while, high
seriousness was a part (only a part) of the mix. No one likes to think
that the vector that has carried him into the demography could
get lost *in* the demography, but that is what happens. Rock and
roll—or the generating spirit of rock and roll—could get lost there,
easily. And just think of all the ideas—and changes—there were
implicit in the hegemony of rock and roll. We could be left with
. . . just some of the music.

Then, when the generating ideas get lost, people who have
forgotten *why* they are singing certain songs begin to hunger for
new generating ideas.

People need to (as one says now) understand the aesthetic of
the 1950s; not just the Fonz or the Avedon fashion photographs,
but the whole landscape. And here, a study of the demography as
it was then, can be a help. There were still active, in 1963, many
men and women whose point of view had been formed *before the
First World War*. *That* was what was really going away then; a powerful generation for whom the landscape was: the real landscape—
and books, was going away for good.

They didn't think of themselves that way, but they were a
powerful part of *the mix*. And I am not just talking about WASPs
here. There was a sense in which new emigrants from Europe,
African-Americans, and old-line WASPs (*anyone*, that is, with
fifteen or twenty years of pre-WWI information under their belts)
had more in common with *one another* than with their own children. What they had in common was that they *didn't* think of
themselves as part of *the mix*; they thought of themselves some
other way.

The history of the media (the years 1941–1945 somewhat aside) has been our history; the history of our, by now, hopelessly conflicted collective personality. I have referred in this essay to my partner and his father. My partner's name was Timothy S. Mayer. He died in 1988. His father is dead now too. Tim died—and he was the *smartest* of men, and among the most talented; he died with no clear view of what had happened to himself culturally, especially within his own family. I remember one Sunday with Tim. As usual, he was *running something down.* It was "Jambalaya," the Hank Williams song. Hank, Tim explained, was riffing off the permanent vogue for *exotica.* He related "Jambalaya" to "Old Cape Cod," the Patti Page song (only Tim could find a link between Hank Williams and Patti Page) and took the whole thing back to "Banks of the Wabash," on the one hand (a turn-of-the-century, I-love-America, bring-tears-to-your-eyes-song) and "Making Wikki-Wakki Down in Waikiki" (jittery 'twenties flapper song). Old Hank, Tim more than implied, was trying to get to a *Hawaiian* energy. And somewhere, right this minute there is a Hawaiian—I mean a real one, descended from a line of Hawaiian kings—wearing a cowboy hat and singing "Lonesome Blues."

This is our Life, and it is supposed to be an attractive one. When people do somewhat serious work (I am thinking of Quentin Tarantino, just now), they riff off *that* energy—a Demonic Gangster standing alone with bloody hands on top of a sacred mountain suddenly breaks into a chorus of "Margaritaville." "Stepped on a pop top," the gangster sings, oblivious both to the blood on his hands and to the beauty around him. But it *is* a Demonic Gangster now who gets caught in Cross Cultural Perspective. *No one* is content just to make Wikki-Wakki down on Waikiki.

Tim knew nearly everything; but he didn't know what had happened to *him.* At the very end of his life, he said a very unrealistic thing about his relationship to his father. He said it to a wise person a little older than he.

"I don't know what you're saying, Tim," the wise person said.

"Right," Tim said in his very beautiful deep voice, "and I don't know what I'm saying."

In America, it is dangerous to know very much—or *anything*. And yet people want to know. I think the best moment in the essay you are about to read was something I got off TV: the moment in which Richard Dawson, the host of a terrible program called *Family Feud*, asked someone what he thought the audience would say the *average* was. No *reality* whatsoever. No *fact* anywhere in sight.

That's real privilege, of course. When you are rewarded for knowing what your fellow citizens are likely to say their delusions are. No pain, all gain. I have never been able to get certain pieces of old common sense out of my mind. Wouldn't the Chinese, to take one example, like to be in that situation; where the whole world revolved around what a Chinese person said a Chinese audience would guess the Chinese average was. Everyone likes no pain, all gain, after all. It doesn't have to be us.

Family Feud is no longer on television. Or at least I haven't seen it recently. I'm glad. I would like to know in what way the producers of this show *aren't* culpable. *I* think they *are* culpable—and to no very interesting end. My guess is that they are making wikki-wakki down in Waikiki, shedding a tear for Old Hank, and wondering how Quentin Tarantino got to his creativity. They go to *Natural Born Killers*, and wish *they* had the status that comes from eviscerating *their* aesthetic. All pain, no gain—culturally, I mean.

I have a New Television Moment to offer up. From the *Sally Jessy Raphael* show. Makes Richard Dawson look like Alistair Cooke. Sally had an all-gossip show recently. Hollywood gossip, New York gossip, gossip about the royals. Then she went into her audience to ask various audience members if they had any questions. Did they want more Hollywood gossip? Did they want more New York gossip? Did they want more about Princess Di and the rugby player? One audience member had seen *Natural Born Killers;* was a little hip; had a sly Quentin Tarantino smile. "Well, Sally," the sly audience member asked, "what's the gossip about *you?*"

And why not give you TV Moment Number Two. Geraldo Rivera (world's most culpable man; I have been drawing back from writing this just to avoid the pain of mentioning his name) is interviewing a panel of Teenage Satanists. As you know, in addition to being the worst person on the face of the earth, Geraldo is just about the *nicest.* A critical word you never get out of Geraldo ("Now, Mr. Teenage Satanist, the reason you're feeling that way, Mr. Teenage Satanist, is that, Mr. Teenage Satanist, your options, Mr. Teenage Satanist, your opportunities for spiritual growth . . ."—well, you never get a critical word). But Geraldo isn't in *favor* of Teenage Satanism; he wouldn't want to leave you with *that* impression. So he is asking the Teenage Satanists if, in fact, they don't think they might not be passing through a *phase.* The Teenage Satanists are quite sure they are happy as they are. Geraldo presses on. Don't they think that *someday*—and he doesn't quite hold out the image of a white picket fence (or a talk show of their own), but his face— his lovely, friendly, prosperous-as-hell face—indicates that all things are possible here in the Land of the Free. This is a little too much for one particularly content Teenage Satanist. He doesn't like the white picket fence in what Geraldo has said. He makes immediate accurate reference to a famous Geraldo incident in which—did he?—Geraldo indicated a kind of sort of interest in the possibilities—are they there?—of the, let us call it, the *occult.* Geraldo piped down. Cut to commercial.

George W. S. Trow

A Brief Essay on Men

Last night I turned on my television here in Haines, Alaska, and found myself watching a CBS documentary on World War I. Really, it was very good. "My God," I thought, "CBS still shows things like this?" Well, of course they don't. The CBS documentary was on the Learning Channel. Good for them—the Learning Channel, that is.

I have always been fascinated by World War I. It was after that event, after all, that our Attention Deficit Syndrome got under way. The Well-Rewarded Jitteryness of—all of it; the speakeasy lifestyle which gave birth to "Broadway Brevities" which led to the New York *Graphic*—I am talking about Walter Winchell here, and the modern tabloid style—which has been the—oh let us call it the *carrier* for the Goat and Adding Machine Ritual in our national life.

So, since I grew up in a seventy-year heritage of the American Jitters, I have always been interested in World War I. I know a lot about it—historically, I mean; the difference between the Kaiser and the Austrian Emperor, and the difference between the English and those two; like that, as they say in the gossip columns. Last night I put all of that aside in my mind. I just kept looking at the *men*. Serbian; Turkish; German; Austrian; Lawrence in the desert with the Arabs. Another version of the human race. Nothing to do with us as we are now. Naturally, that is an accepted fact. But does it have to come down to a choice between Geraldo and the Teenage Satanist? How about another choice, another *opportunity*?

My Way of Surviving

I survived and my partner died. I think I survived because I have known since I was seven years old how a newspaper is made.

A Fact

A child will have seen upward of four thousand hours of television before he or she ever sees a school. This is as much time as that child will spend in his or her high-priced college classroom—should he or she ever get to a high-priced college classroom.

An Overview—for a Puzzled, Intelligent European

The tradition of Washington *ended* on May 7, 1945.

An Explanation—for the Young Male Child I Saw in Douglas, Alaska

Your parents had a third parent—television. If you went back to 1950, you would be surprised. Many people—of all kinds and conditions—had just two parents.

In the time since then, the referee has won all the championship matches—and the referee is a value-free ritual.

A Motto—for the Young Male Child I Saw in Douglas, Alaska

Perhaps you will need a motto. I suggest this one: "Wounded by the Million; Healed—One by One."

Within the Context
of No Context

Wonder

Wonder was the grace of the country. Any action could be justified by that: the wonder it was rooted in. Period followed period, and finally the wonder was *that things could be built so big*. Bridges, skyscrapers, *fortunes*, all having a life first in the marketplace, still drew on the force of wonder. But then a moment's quiet. What was it now that was built so big? Only the marketplace itself. Could there be wonder in that? The size of the con?

History

That movement, from wonder to the wonder that a country should be so big, to the wonder that a building could be so big, to the last, small wonder, that a marketplace could be so big—that was the movement of history. Then there was a change. The direction of the movement paused, sat silent for a moment, and reversed. From that moment, vastness was the start, not the finish. The movement now began with the fact of two hundred million, and the move-

43

ment was toward a unit of one, alone. Groups of more than one were now united not by a common history but by common characteristics. History became the history of demographics, the history of no-history.

History
History has been the record of growth, conflict, and destruction.

The New History
The New History was the record of the expression of demographically significant preferences: the lunge of demography *here* as opposed to *there*.

The Decline of Adulthood
In the New History, nothing was judged—only counted. The power of judging was then subtracted from what it was necessary for a man to learn to do. In the New History, the preferences of a child carried as much weight as the preferences of an adult, so the refining of preferences was subtracted from what it was necessary for a man to learn to do. In the New History, the ideal became *agreement* rather than well-judged action, so men learned to be competent only in those modes which embraced the possibility of agreement. The world of power changed. What was powerful grew more powerful in ways that could be easily measured, grew less powerful in every way that could not be measured.

Powerful Men
The most powerful men were those who most effectively used the power of adult competence to enforce childish agreements.

Television

Television is the force of no-history, and it holds the archives of the history of no-history. Television is a mystery. Certain of its properties are known, though. It has a *scale*. The scale *does not vary*. The trivial is raised up to the place where this scale has its home; the powerful is lowered there. In the place where this scale has its home, childish agreements can be arrived at and enforced effectively— childish agreements, and agreements wearing the mask of childhood.

Television

Television has a scale. It has other properties, but what television has to a dominant degree is a certain scale and the power to enforce it. No one has been able to describe the scale as it is experienced. We know some of its properties, though.

Television does not vary. The trivial is raised up to power in it. The powerful is lowered toward the trivial.

The power behind it resembles the power of no-action, the powerful passive.

It is *bewitching*.

It interferes with growth, conflict, and destruction, and these forces are different in its presence.

"Entertainment" is an unsatisfactory word for what it encloses or projects or makes possible.

No good has come of it.

False History

For a while, a certain voice continued. *Booming*. As though history were still a thing done by certain men in a certain place. It was embarrassing. To a person growing up in the power of demography, this voice was foolish.

45

The Aesthetic of the Hit
To a person growing up in the power of demography, it was clear that history had to do not with the powerful actions of certain men but with the processes of choice and preference.

The Aesthetic of the Hit
The power shifted. In the phrase "I Like Ike," the power shifted. It shifted from General Eisenhower to someone called Ike, who embodied certain aspects of General Eisenhower and certain aspects of affection for General Eisenhower. Then it shifted again. From "Ike," you could see certain aspects of General Eisenhower. From "like," all you could see was other Americans engaged in a process resembling the processes of intimacy. This was a comfort.

The Aesthetic of the Hit
The comfort was in agreement, the easy exercise of the modes of choice and preference. It was attractive and, as it was presented, not difficult. But, once interfered with, the processes of choice and preference began to take on an uncomfortable aspect. Choice in respect to important matters became more and more difficult; people found it troublesome to settle on a mode of work, for instance, or a partner. Choice in respect to trivial matters, on the other hand, assumed an importance that no one could have thought to predict. So what happened then was that important forces that fell outside the new scale of national life (which was the life of television), began to find a home in the exercise of preference concerning trivial matters, so that attention, aspiration, even affection came to adhere to shimmers thrown up by the demography in trivial matters. The attraction of inappropriate attention, aspiration, and affection to a *shimmer*

spins out, in its operation, a little mist of energy which is rather like love, but trivial, rather like a sense of home, but apt to disappear. In this mist exists the Aesthetic of the Hit.

Membership

The middle distance fell away, so the grids (from small to large) that had supported the middle distance fell into disuse and ceased to be understandable. Two grids remained. The grid of two hundred million and the grid of intimacy. Everything else fell into disuse. There was a national life—a *shimmer* of national life—and intimate life. The distance between these two grids was very great. The distance was very frightening. People did not want to measure it. People began to lose a sense of what distance was and of what the usefulness of distance might be.

~ ~ ~

Distance

Because the distance between the grids was so great, there was less in the way of comfort. The middle distance had been a comfort. But the middle distance had fallen away. The grid of national life was very large now, but the space in which one man felt at home shrank. It shrank to intimacy.

Intimacy

It followed that people were comfortable only with the language of intimacy. Whatever business was done had to be done in that language. The language of "You are not alone." How else would a person know? The language of intimacy spread. It was meant to be reassuring. But during the same period, in a most upsetting way, real intimacy came to seem to be a kind of affliction.

Pseudo-Intimacy

Things very distant came powerfully close, but just for a minute. It was a comfort. And useful to men who wished to enforce childish agreements, because the progress of the *advertisement* is toward the destruction of distance between the product and the person who might consume the product.

Loneliness

It was sometimes lonely in the grid of one, alone. People reached out toward their home, which was in television. They looked for help.

Celebrities

Celebrities have an intimate life and a life in the grid of two hundred million. For them, there is no distance between the two grids in American life. Of all Americans, only they are complete.

Celebrities

The most successful celebrities are products. Consider the real role in American life of Coca-Cola. Is any man as well loved as this soft drink is?

Celebrities

A product consumed by a man alone in a room exists in the grid of one, alone and in the grid of two hundred million. To the man alone, it is a comfort. But just for a minute.

Comfort

Comfort *failed*. Who would have thought that it could fail? People felt teased by a promise of a national life that did not arrive and an intimacy that could not be consummated. So *teased*.

The Problem

So one or two of the babies began to experience a problem. Loneliness rose to the surface. It was a problem. No exit for the babies. Dead end for the babies. It was a problem. And *new*. A problem is a disease in the demography. A difficulty is something overcome by a man—or not. A *problem* is something enjoyed by a piece of the demography. "I'm just a Hoosier." No. No one cares. "I am Youth." Better. "I am a battered child." Very good.

~ ~ ~

The Decline of Adulthood

During the 1960s, there was conflict between the generation born during (and soon after) the Second World War and the generation born during (and soon after) the First World War. There was also a debate. Although the debate was supposed to be candid, some truths were avoided—almost shyly. Much of the debate had to do with power and the abuse of power, but no one ever asked if the men in positions of control who were being confronted with evidence of their abuse of power had any right to be considered powerful in the first place. No one inquired into the nature of the connection between the men who had fashioned conventional white society and the men of forty or fifty or sixty who were its contemporary stewards. No one asked if in fact *any connection existed at all*. A continuum of power was assumed (perhaps out of instinctive politeness or instinctive fear), and what was debated was the question of its abuse. In some instances, the assumed continuum was stretched to include members of the younger generation, with remarkable results.

The Decline of Adulthood

During the 1960s, a young black man in a university class described the Dutch painters of the seventeenth century as "belonging" to the white students in the room, and not to him. This idea was seized on by white members of the class. They acknowledged that they were at one with Rembrandt. They acknowledged their dominance. They offered to discuss, at any length, their inherited power to oppress. It was thought at the time that reactions of this type had to do with "white guilt" or "white masochism." No. No. It was white *euphoria*. Many, many white children of that day felt the power of their inheritance for the first time in the act of rejecting it, and they insisted on rejecting it and rejecting it and rejecting it, so that they might continue to feel the power of that connection. Had the young black man asked, "Who is this man to you?" the pleasure they felt would have vanished in embarrassment and resentment.

The Decline of Adulthood

"Adulthood" in the last generations has had very little to do with "adulthood" as that word would have been understood by adults in any previous generation. Rather, "adulthood" has been defined as "a position of control in the world of childhood."

The Adolescent Orthodoxy

Ambitious Americans, sensing this, have preferred to remain adolescents, year after year.

The Authority of No-Authority
A child watching television will not encounter a discussion of how he might marry or how he might work, but he will find material relating to how he should be honest in coming to terms with his divorce, and he will encounter much material that has as the source of its energy his confusion and unhappiness.

Scale
The permission given by television is permission to make tiny choices, within the context of total permission infected with a sense of no permission at all.

Permission
An important role of a father is to give a son a sense of permission—a sense of what might be done. This still works, but since no adult is supported by the voice of the culture (which is now a childish voice), it does not work well.

~ ~ ~

Experts
In the absence of adults, people came to put their trust in *experts*.

Experts
Only an *expert* can deal with a problem. Only an expert or a pleasant man on television with access to experts. Only an expert or a man on television who knows how to welcome an expert or a prob-

lem or love for a problem. An expert or a man on television or—in certain cases, an expert trained in the modes of action—a *matron*. In the age of no-authority, these are the authorities.

Important Programming
Important programming is programming that recognizes the problem.

Important Programming
If it is just a problem—teen-age alcoholics who need to talk to Matron—then it is a little boring after a while, because it is only one-half of the problem. Then the problem might have to be doubled. You might have to add Angel Dust or Runaways or Child Abuse. You might have to, because just the problem is only half of the problem.

Series
Or you might stick it in a series. Let Quincy deal with the problem. Quincy is *so angry*. Quincy *hates* kiddie porn. Quincy gets angry at the idea that anyone could even contemplate the exploitation of children. Just ask him.

Series
But it's still just half of the problem. Even if Pepper dresses up like a whore to stop whores from turning babies into whores, it's still just half of the problem.

Experts
The problem is offered up to authority for healing. But Pepper shies away from healing, and so does Matron. They conduct the problem to other experts. The experts shy away a little, too. Who would

have thought it? "We move toward a full discussion of the problem," they murmur. "During this discussion, you will experience a little sense of *home*. Do you feel it now? No? Then perhaps our discussion has not been full. Is that perhaps *your fault*?"

"In what lies your authority?" a willfull person asks after a time.

"Why, in the problem," an expert answers honestly.

Important Programming

The most important programming deals with people with a serious problem who make it to the Olympics. It is the powerful metaphor of our time—babies given up for dead who struggle toward national life and make it just for a minute. It's a long distance to come. People feel it very deeply and cheer the babies on.

Problems

An important question to ask about an association of individuals is, "How does it spend its best energies?" One can imagine many answers to this question. One answer, certainly, would be "Dealing with problems." One would expect this answer from, for instance, a poor association of individuals or an association without ambition. But even from associations as impoverished as these associations might be, one would not expect the answer "Aspiring to love problems."

Adolescence

The *New York Times Book Review* published an interview with a woman whose novel had been given the place of honor in the *Book Review* that week. Her novel, according to the *Times*, traced a woman called Vida through her years in the Movement. Of the Movement, the author of the novel remembered this:

> I remember walking around with other organizers and fanta-sizing about what we would do after the revolution with all the buildings, what human uses they could be put to. What marvelous daycare centers and hospices they would become.

This woman was talking about New York City. Her idea had been that the revolution would bring better parks to New York, and beautiful places to live, and day-care centers, and hospices. Her idea was that New York should be *human*. Now, this is simply a mistake. New York is an inhuman machine put together to serve the most ambitious interests of a certain part of American secular society. It has human aspects, because human needs must be met before ambitions can proceed toward realization, but the fulfillment of those human needs is an uninteresting precondition of the life of the ambitions. In human terms, there is no reason to live in New York, and if New York were to become a city in which day-care centers and hospices were the dominant institutions it would soon be depopulated.

The Cold Child

The people who undertook revolutionary activities knew one thing: they knew warm from cold. Not a small thing to know. They saw that the power of the adult world had hidden behind masks and that the masks were fashioned from a pseudo-cheerfulness which was essentially cold. They came to understand that they had been cheated. They did not understand, however, what they had been cheated *of*. As their orthodoxy began to form, it cohered around the idea of the *warm child*.

The Adolescent Orthodoxy

The adolescent orthodoxy is the orthodoxy of growth, of becoming, of awkward search. It has embraced the most ambitious energies of the society since the mode of the cold child was established on television. It has as its aim the undoing of the work of the cold child. It is carried out in mourning for lost childhood. Its eye is always there—on childhood.

The Cold Child

Television is dangerous because it operates according to an attention span that is childish but is cold. It simulates the warmth of a childish response but is cold. If it were completely successful in simulating the warmth of childish enthusiasm—that is, if it were warm—would that be better? It would be better only in a society that had agreed that childish warmth and spontaneity were equivalent to public virtue; that is, in a society of children.

What is a cold child? A sadist. What is childish behavior that is cold? It is sadism. After generations of cold childhood, cold childhood upon cold childhood, one piling on the other, moving, *at their best,* into frenzied adolescence, certain ugly blemishes have surfaced. An overt interest in sadism, for instance, and an interest in unnatural children. Americans, unrooted, blow with the wind, but they feel the truth when it touches them. An interest in sadism is an interest in truth in that it exposes the processes of false affection. A horror of children is the natural result of the spread, across the grid, of a cold childhood.

The Cold Child

As the mode of the cold child continues and the aesthetics of pseudo-intimacy become so widely accepted that forms of behavior are forgotten which require an understanding of what distance there is between different people at different moments—as this continues, it has been possible for the proprietors of the commercial culture to create certain new masks out of material that was thrown up by the "rebellious" adolescent orthodoxy. Out of daycare centers and hospices, for instance. The cold child is happy to embrace the warm child. Both, after all, make a point of *smiling*.

The Cold Child

There is another possibility. It is possible to *embrace* the cold child, after all. To *accept* the corruption in his smile. Some artists and some terrorists have seen the space made ready for this possibility. They are quite candid that their interest is in *defacement*. Certain artists, certain terrorists, and, of course, very many children.

Smiles

Look at the girl smile! The more she smiles, the more certain it is that she represents something trivial, something shocking, or something failed.

~ ~ ~

Distance

The background is distant, the sense of protection is distant—so people feel completely protected and completely unprotected at the same time.

Distance

The background is distant, the sense of protection is distant. People are so frightened. There is so much distance between them and their protection. They reward anyone who can convince them that there is no distance.

Distance

In the vast distance between the protection and the protected, there is space for mirages of pseudo-intimacy. It is in this space that celebrities dance.

False Prophets

And, since the dancing celebrities occupy no real space, there is room for other novel forms to take hold. Some of these are really very strange.

~ ~ ~

Failure

No one, now, minds a con man. But no one likes a con man who doesn't know what we think we want.

Winning

When the idea of winning is empty, men of integrity may fill it up. When it is full, but empty of integrity, then the only interest is in disappointment.

~ ~ ~

People

People. So many people. Everywhere you look: on the streets; in the stores; queuing up for a little treat. It's a glut of people. So many. But not everyone, of course. Sometimes it's everyone, though. HEY, AMERICA. That's one group. It's a group of people. Not a small group—not by any means. It's not everyone, though—not the old-sters and the welfare cheats. Well, sometimes it's the oldsters, too, and the welfare cheats, but not often. During the news, for instance, it's oldsters. Oldsters get special attention then. *Mom's incredible. Sometimes, when her hands knot up in a kind of nineteenth-century pain, sometimes, when her shuffling steps bring stab after stab, sometimes; even then, we let her make the breakfast.* Most of the time, though, when we say HEY, AMERICA, it's a smaller group we have in mind.

People. So many people. *Too* many people. Sometimes it's a little crowded. How many? Unclear. More than two hundred mil-lion? How do you arrive at that figure? Do you go from house to house—houses formed into little units, constituting parts, then, of larger units, which are, in turn, parts of larger units, until you get to units large enough to count on the fingers of one hand? Or do you start instead with the two hundred million and slice it up? There's a difference. Taken from one direction, people have per-sonal histories. Taken from the other, they have characteristics. Taken in one way, little units have small histories or, sometimes, histories unexpectedly large; taken in the other way, they have characteristics. Large units—the large units resulting from the way a thing grows, step by step, year by year—have history, the record of the independent action of growing from small to large. But only from the direction of small to large. From the other direction, the direction of two hundred million sliced up, they have a share. Tak-ing apart the share, you find characteristics. Agglomerating the characteristics so that they will stand on their own, so that you have something distinct to say about this share, as opposed to that share, you resort to sociology.

New England is history. Step One. Step Two. Do this. Do that. This happened. That happened. It all adds up to New England. It doesn't break down from something else. It is no share of anything larger. History takes a certain course, and it *adds up* to New England. Of course, once it does, you can work it in other ways. New England as a phrase means a certain thing, because certain things have added up to mean New England. But once a phrase means a certain thing, you can abuse the meaning and twist it: refer to the sense of what "New England" means to suit your purposes, which may not have correct reference to the history of New England—which may, in fact, directly oppose the essence of that history. SHOT OF FABULOUS OLD NEW ENGLAND INN. Look at the clapboards. So white. Look at that *porch*. So like New England, that porch. *Why, Mrs. Martin, you're pouring Silt-Whip over that old New England cherry cobbler. Of course it's Silt-Whip; nothing else is good enough for Martin's Inn.* At a certain moment, Mrs. Martin would have been whipped herself. A certain stern New England man would have taken her out and beaten her. And sent her out of town. But not now. She stands on the porch of her fabulous New England inn with her artificial dessert topping, made from lard, engine oil, preservatives extracted from offal and animal screams. *Why is she there? Liaison.* She's doing liaison work. She stands on a little pivot. It's history. What she is is the purveyor of a motif. In her case, the motif is history used in the service of the force of no-history, and no-history is the force of the share, and the characteristics of the share, and the grid of two hundred million.

What is it? It's *television*. It's a program *on* television. A little span of time. How does it work? It's a little span of time made friendly by repetition. In a way, it doesn't exist at all. Just what does, then? A certain ability to transmit and receive and then to apply layers of affection and longing and doubt. Two abilities: to do a very complex kind of work, involving electrons, and then to cover the coldness of that with a hateful familiarity. Why hateful? Because it hasn't anything to do with a human being as a human being is strong. It has to do with a human being as a human being is weak and willing to be fooled: the human being's eagerness to perceive as warm something that is cold, for instance; his eagerness to be a part of what one cannot be a part of, to love what cannot be loved. What is it? It's family hour. What is it? It's a *program*, a little slice of time during which a man and his wife and a woman who works for him sit together behind a little desk-like thing. What do they do? They answer questions. Not questions about France, or the Battle of Britain, or what American women despise most about their husbands according to the editors of *Modern Maiden*. What, then? About what? Together, in discomfort, they answer questions designed to awaken discomfort. In this way, a little reality can be got to. You can see it on their faces. They are uncomfortable, longing for comfort. The questions make them uncomfortable, and they recognize being uncomfortable as referring to their reality. They take comfort in this reference. In that, and in the fact that they are in public. Out of their small family, which may not exist, so lonely is it, and into the grid of two hundred million.

The host is Jim Peck. So friendly, Jim Peck. He has curly hair. Fornication is what he has on his mind as he does his job. Fornication as it has reference to the little units of man, wife, woman working for the man. But no real fornication. Nothing to do with real fornication. Nothing like "Jessica, has Harold fornicated with Monica at the office?" The questions are conditional, referring to what the man will say. Prizes are awarded to wives or female employees according to their ability to guess what the man will say. It forms a littl grid. A little *context*. Convincing while it lasts, but dirty. Shimmering with doubt and embarrassment. Why is it allowed? Because the embarrassment forms a context. The comfort of discomfort. The comfort of reality, which is a reality of discomfort. And *interest*. That there should be in their own sadness the means to form a little event within a context. Nobody does anything in America unless it is perceived as a step up. As the boy slices his skin to watch a scar form, he thinks how loathsome and intolerable life was before he thought to do it, and how comforting it is to belong to the new aristocracy of people who have had the imagination to have an intention to wound themselves.

Teen-Age Alcoholism

Who is he? He's a man in business. Watch him walk. Down the hall. A smile on his face. What is it? A new *problem*. For a while, it was a new smile that counted, or a new thrill. Now, in certain parts of the building, what matters is the problem, and the little frown of recognition when the problem is mentioned, and the little stabs of pain when a baby girl or a baby boy is shown to have the problem. What matters is that, and the effective invocation of a therapeutic orthodoxy as people come together to talk about the problem. So openly! They talk about the problem just as if it were a menu! Or a date on the calendar, or a treat! They learn from an *expert* to talk. They didn't know how. Matron tells them how. "Did you know that Baby Judy was gulping twenty Quaaludes a day?" Matron is worried. Matron knows how to talk. She learned it in school. She knows how to talk. *In a way*. She knows everything *in a way*. She is the midwife of the problem, an important person. Matron is here to persuade us that *someone knows what to do*. Matron is here to say that open and honest *dialogue* will help keep Baby Judy from gulping Quaaludes and drinking Night Train Express and marking her arm with razor blades.

Matron is important. She's one of the most important people in the whole world. She knows about Teen-Age Alcoholism and Drug-Related Deaths and Child Abuse and Wife-Beating and every other problem. She's here to help. In public. On the channels. On the special programs and in the context of a series. Ask Matron. She's the expert. She has taken courses. She didn't know a thing for a while, but then she took courses, in a school made of cinder block. She knows a crisis. She knows crisis intervention. She doesn't know about daily life, but daily life isn't coherent, so why should she know about it? Who can grasp something that's not coherent? Not Matron. That's why she sticks to a problem.

The problem comes with a lie. Matron gags on it. The problem goes down easily, but the lie sticks. In a quiet moment, perhaps as she takes a drink, Matron begins to wonder. Not about her school. Matron hated her school. She was clear about that from the start. Not about Baby Judy. Baby Judy is the most boring person in the world—anyone could tell. At home, in a quiet moment, Matron wonders. She wonders what it is that bothers her; she wonders if it's time for another drink; she wonders if it would be interesting to mark up her arm with razor blades.

Teen-Age Alcoholism

The lie is in this—that the teen-age alcoholic suffers from a problem in the foreground, a problem within a context, liable to solution within the frame of the context, subject to powers of arrangement near to the hand of the organizing power of the context. The reality is this—that the problem is the only context available to the people in the problem.

Contexts

Art requires a context: the power of this moment, the moment of the events in the foreground, seen against the accumulation of other moments. The moment in the foreground adheres to the accumulation or rejects it briefly before joining it. How do the manipulators of television deal with this necessity?

1. By the use of false love. The love engendered by familiarity. False love is the Aesthetic of the Hit. What is loved is a hit. What is a hit is loved. The back-and-forth of this establishes a context. It seems powerful. What could be more powerful? The love of tens of millions of people. It's a Hit! Love it! It's a Hit. It loves you because you love it because it's a Hit! This is a powerful context, with a most powerful momentum. But what? It stops in a second. The way love can stop, but quicker. It's not love. There is a distance so great between the lovers that no contact is ever made that is not an abstract contact.

2. By the use of abandoned shells. Pepper dresses up like a cop. Pepper dresses up like a hooker. Pepper has to dress up like a cop to dress up like a hooker. Now This. It's about cowboys! It's about doctors! It's about cowboys who want to become doctors. Or lawyers! Or *young lawyers*. Or girls who want to dress up like lawyers or like a city lawyer coming to the frontier who finds that the law isn't what it seems to be when he finds out *Jenny's blind.*

3. By the use of ad hoc contexts. Just for the moment. We're here together, in a little house. It makes such good sense. But just for a moment. We're playing Password! Do you remember when we played Password! Do you remember Johnny? Yes, you do. When he squirted whipped cream on Burt Reynolds, into his trousers? Remember that? Now This.

Problems

They merge. They mate. They are seen in different combinations. The city lawyer who comes to the frontier and finds that the law isn't what it seems to be inhabits an abandoned hovel remaining from the time when popular entertainment dealt with history or a gloss on history, with adult experience or a gloss on adult experience. Why is he in that hovel? Because the program needs some little bit of organization or it will fall apart before the commercial break. The best organization is false love. Loving Mork from Ork is the best way to get to the commercial, but it's hard. *You can't get them to love just anyone.* You can't get people to believe that they already love just anyone. You can't get them to believe that everyone else is already loving just anyone. You have to start with what they do feel and tease it toward love. *Interest* first, novelty, skin-popping little bits of abandoned reality, building a little house out of that until it's comfortable. Then bring the comfort to the surface. "You're so comfortable! It's almost like love!" It's almost like something you remember. But not the negative side of what you remember. Just the part you liked. Not the boring parts. Remember, he's a doctor only because you like a doctor. He's a lawyer because you like a lawyer; of course you also don't like a lawyer, so we left those parts out. Not completely out. An edge of what you don't like in a lawyer, but he's going to find that the law isn't what it seems to be, he's going to find out that the law is more like what *you* think it is! He's going to learn that the law is warm and human and caring, because Jenny's *blind.* Wearing shreds of abandoned adulthood, moving through a landscape of ill-remembered history, piecing little bits of reality together, this ill-remembered shard together with that one, the city lawyer encounters something very contemporary in its glow—a problem. A person with a problem. Notice how it is, how it's changed. Melodrama from the beginning of time has shown the orphaned and the blind and the lame. Melodramas have shown the pathos in the condition of these people, and in their loneliness. The important moment has been this: the orphan peeking through the window at the happy family together around the fire. The problem of the melodrama has been this: to bring the child into the circle around the fire. The circle exists, the fire exists, the child exists; the only question is whether circumstances will allow the child to be reconciled with the community. In the television story, which is not a melodrama but a momentary fabric from outer space, with no direct connection to even those easy aspects of human perception upon which the melodrama played—in the television story, *the lonely child creates the circle.* The affliction spins the context. To a problem, like blindness or drug addiction or cancer, to a simple state of trouble—to that state there adheres more reality than adheres to the ragged patching of abandoned realities that costume the city lawyer on the frontier.

Each new birth of reality, however deformed, can be exploited in its turn. Movies are best at this. Movies are the gloss on television, and on the world created by television. To the extent that they comment on the blemishes rising to the surface of the world created by television, they are big movies. *Apocalypse Now* is not so much a movie about Vietnam as it is a movie about the world created by television. *The Exorcist* and a hundred other movies openly admit the horror of the American cold childhood. Movies like *Jaws* and *Animal House* and *Star Wars* are powerful because they operate within a warm childishness, and thus constitute a release from the cold tease of television.

Magazines in the Age of Television

Magazines are based on agreements. Some of these agreements are simple: "This magazine will report on events in the world of tennis." Some of these agreements appear for a moment to be simple but are not: "This magazine will report on events in the world of tennis but will but will but will but will do more." In the second instance, you look at the agreement and you see simple words: "report" and "tennis." The rest is hard to follow. There is a modification, a little dance, and a promise. It is seductive, possibly, and a little nervous. What is the real agreement to which the reader is asked to subscribe? Maybe it is this: "This magazine will appear to report on events in the world of tennis but will in fact strive to make the reader envy and seek to emulate a certain group of people, who will be made to appear to be at ease in the world of tennis." Maybe it is even this: "This magazine will seek to make its readers uncomfortable by the calculated use of certain icons associated with tennis, so that the readers will turn, for comfort, to the products advertised in our pages and buy them."

To edit a magazine that seeks to report, objectively, on events in the world of tennis is not ambitious, perhaps, but it is not ungenerous. The editors will share with their readers some knowledge that the readers do not possess. The transaction is straightforward; money and attention from the reader; knowledge from the editors. If the transaction is completed successfully, month after month, year after year, a beneficial thing will occur: a rhythm and a trust will be established between the editors and the readers, and both groups will begin to bring more to the exchange than they did at the start, which is to say that each will bring the history of the relationship to the relationship as it unfolds. For the editors, the gift of history will be the natural formation of a certain authority; for the readers, the gift will be the comfort of trust. Nothing like this will occur in the case of the magazine based on a deceptive or convoluted agreement. In this case, no natural context will grow, because the nature of the real transaction cannot be revealed without endangering the context of false authority which the editors have sought to establish.

There are very few simple magazines now; that is, very few magazines that seek to establish a simple, honorable agreement with the reader. It has been some time since there has been a *simple fashion magazine*, for instance—one in which the wearing of certain clothes by certain people has been of any importance. Instead, what has been going on for some time is that what there is in a fashion magazine is something to do with the idea of the possible existence of approval and disapproval adhering to clothes, in an abstract way that shifts and runs before the reader with a completely confusing result. What has been going on for some time is that what a fashion magazine advances is not the idea that there is one interesting thing to do or wear but the idea that there are a hundred and one possibilities existing together in a context that is never described, so that what shifts is *not the clothes in the foreground* (which was what shifted before) *but the background itself,* which is never shown, because it is shifting in a way that the editors cannot possibly describe but that they pretend to know, because that is what their effort has been founded on—that they do know it. This has been going on for some time, and yet fashion magazines have been more successful than ever, until they have approached the context of a Hit: they are advertised in because they are advertised in.

Duplicity is surrounded by a nervous strength. That is its charm. The charm lasts for just a moment, but it does last for a moment and is powerful in that moment. A slot machine is interesting, for example, and a con man spinning a story. These things create a context. It's like *home,* but just for a moment. Little windows. The possibilities are cherries, bells, other things, but no things other than the ones that are there. It is comfortable. But the comfort goes away quickly. A man approaches on the street, and then a woman. They are attentive. They have a story. Attentiveness is a comfort. The context of a story is seductive. Is it greed that draws one on? Possibly. But there are a hundred ways to be greedy. Of the ways to be greedy, surely *shrewdly* is the best. But it is not acting shrewdly to put one's hope in a slot machine or in two strangers. What is it? Acting gullibly? Possibly. Yet this is not a time in which there is much gullibility or innocence or trust straight from the country. Indeed, everyone is agreed that it is a time of grim sophistication. But the times are good for gambling and for strangers on the road. Why should that be? Possibly because con games offer a kind of sense, a kind of context, a kind of home. The kind of home we have begun to think of *as* home.

What begins to appear is a hunger for authority—but authority of a particular kind. Authority that requires submission—but just for a minute. Authority that gives a sense of home—but just for a minute. It is an authority that wants to give you something—but not right now. *We can't do it right now. It will take a while before we can, but it will be great when we can, and we can because you can, because we need a little more and you have a little more; that's it—just a little more from you, then you can have it all!*

It begins to appear that a magazine, instead of depending for its success on the successful completion of a straightforward transaction, can depend on the energy generated in the reader by *noncompletion.* It begins to appear that, provided the magazine is skillfully run, it will do no harm if the reader comes to suspect that he is involved in a transaction that he does not fully understand. It may be that occasional glimpses into the ambiguity of his position will serve to *fascinate* him, and that his sense that a transaction has been incomplete will lead him to continue to look at the magazine with interest. It may be that the success of certain magazines *depends upon* the ability of the editors successfully to stimulate doubt, to create an atmosphere of unsureness. This is not easy. No powerful accomplishment is easy. It's not easy to get a woman to withdraw money from the bank and give it to a stranger; it's not easy to get fifty million people to think of Suzanne Somers as a beautiful young woman. In life, every powerful accomplishment is hard. Just because it's not worth doing doesn't mean it won't go wrong.

Gossip

In August 1976, the magazine *Esquire* (before it became *Esquire Fortnightly*, which is what it was before it became merely *Esquire* again) published an issue with this announcement on the cover:

GOSSIP SO HOT WE HAD
TO SEAL THE PAGES

Inside the magazine, beginning at page 59, there was a section dealing with the subject of gossip and gossip-writing which required that the reader take some instrument to an uncut page before he could read what the editors of *Esquire* had arranged to tell him. On the cover page of the "sealed" section, there was a photograph of a sleek young woman who wore a red dress with a dotted line down the middle, and the same motif (the dotted line) appeared at the edge of the page that had been "sealed." Instructions on this page read:

Come and get it, America! If you are not home, take this
magazine home. Then take a knife and cut very neatly along
the perforated edge at right. Inside are fourteen pages of what
everybody's talking about. Don't peek into the pages from top
or bottom. Nobody likes a snoop.

It was not difficult to cut the "sealed" page, and it was very easy quickly to read what was inside. What was more difficult was to find the purpose of the effort. Was it a section of real gossip? Was the section critical of gossip? Was it critical of the process of exploiting gossip? Was it finding fun in gossip or in the possibility of exploiting gossip or in the possibility of criticizing the exploitation of gossip? The section denied nothing, admitted nothing. It was lightly here at one moment and there at another. Within the section, there were a thousand small foreground figures moving in confusion against a shifting background. First, there was a list. *Esquire*, in all its incarnations, has liked to avail itself of lists. Lists of funny things. Lists of little pieces of funny things. Lists of things that sound funny when they're juxtaposed with other things. Lists of names that create an effect. Lists of names that create an effect when they're put next to other names or to funny things or to things that might be funny or might be serious. Lists that make use of funny categories or unexpected categories, or categories that sound funny or unexpected when they're juxtaposed with certain things that might be funny or might be serious or might get hold of a nerve. This list seemed to be critical of gossip at some moments:

A Terrible Idea
Whose Time Has Come
People magazine

An Even Worse Idea
Whose Time Has Come
National Enquirer

At other moments, the list seemed to be quite straightforward in its interest in parsing the world of the privileged, as when it named restaurants favored by privileged people in New York, Washington, Chicago, Los Angeles, and San Francisco. At one moment, the compilers contrived a category of "Gossips Posing as Journalists," and they implied that it was not a good thing to be a gossip posing as a journalist; yet revealed through the page like a rash rising through the flesh was the probability that the compilers were themselves gossips posing as journalists. *I'm a lady and I'm going to list all the different kinds of whores. There's this whore and that whore. Don't you love whores? There's this whore and that whore and this one who pretends to be a lady. Isn't that funny? Aren't ladies dumb? But I'm a lady. Are you sure I'm a lady? Of course I'm a lady. I'm a lady because I know what a whore does. I know the way a whore walks into the Beverly Hills Hotel. Don't you love the Beverly Hills Hotel? Don't you love the way they know me at the Beverly Hills Hotel? Don't you love the way you feel when you don't know if I like you or not? Don't you love the way you feel when you don't know if you want to be a whore or not? Would you like to be a whore? Would you like to have me arrange for you to be a whore? Am I arranging it now?*

So it is possible that the benefits of history—which are manifested in the growth of context and in the proper sense of background and foreground—are not available at the moment, because no one now wants to make himself foolish by pretending to know what a background might be or what might constitute a context.

Magazines in the Age of Television

There is very little gossip now. This is thought to be an age of gossip, but that is because people know that it is a small time and they assume that the small things they hear discussed are gossip because they feel, correctly, that the things they hear and want to hear and insist on hearing are beneath history. What is not realized is that the age is beneath gossip, too—that most of what is spoken of as gossip cannot aspire to that title but is, rather, synthetic talk, contrived to meet a supposed need for talk, as television programs are contrived to meet a supposed need for entertainment.

Gossip depends on violation. If it does not provide a sense of violation, it does not exist. When gossip involves a high violation, it comes close to being history. If the violation rests on a simple human impulse that would not be remarked on in an ordinary human being but is perceived as a violation because of the very high station of the figure who is revealed as possessing it, it will overpower the public imagination. The romance between Edward VIII and Mrs. Simpson was the source of the best gossip of this century. The gossip had a foreground of violation and a background of dignity, and the violation was an ordinary action. And also this: the story gave form to the powerful urge that flowed into this century from the nineteenth century and is only now beginning to recede— the urge to shed any context perceived as inhibiting and in conflict with the possibility of personal satisfaction. And also this: the story gave form to the ambiguity of motives adhering to any transaction that involves the shedding of a powerful context, for no one doubted that it was the context of kingship which attracted Mrs. Simpson to her husband. And also this: the story gave form to the question of the real condition of contexts supposedly powerful, for no one doubted that Edward VIII found in his relationship with Mrs. Simpson a context more powerful and more necessary than the context of British history, of which he was the manifest representative.

It is recognized that the magazine *People* is an important contemporary magazine. It is sometimes criticized as purveying *gossip*. It does not purvey gossip. Nor do most "gossip columns" purvey gossip (with its attendant sense of violation)—not in the way that Walter Winchell once did, for example. Instead, *People*, like most of the efforts in print that reflect its concern with celebrities, provides an ad hoc context within which may be placed, each week, certain scraps of synthetic talk which have been judged to have the power to reinforce the ad hoc context so that the ad hoc context may, for a moment, seem to exist. What is the function of synthetic talk enclosed within the ad hoc context of *People*? It is to unite, for a moment, the two remaining grids in American life—the intimate grid and the grid of two hundred million. This is achieved by discussing the intimate life of celebrities who have their home in the grid of two hundred million and by raising up to national attention certain experiences of Americans as they live, lonely, in the grid of intimacy. A subsidiary activity is to report on events taking place within certain eccentric contexts (like the context of an odd sporting event) or to report on quite straightforward events (in the world of science or medicine, for instance) as though they had taken place within an eccentric context. All this is, of course, within the mode of the television talk program—the most effective of all ad hoc contexts. It is difficult to translate into print. How is the translating done? By skill, first of all, and then through the evocation of a voice, a *breath* of a voice—not loud enough to be heard but with sufficient force to be felt in the ear. What is the nature of the voice? It is the voice of American assurance, and of a certain sense of history. It is the voice, reduced to a whisper, of the magazine *Life* as it was under Henry Luce.

It is the idea of *People* to treat its material as if it were history and, what is more, as if it were the history of a happy period. Thus, the self-loathing induced by a surfeit of synthetic talk is overcome. Also the awkward question occasioned by a surfeit of synthetic talk: Where is the substance in this talk? Where is the dignity that this is meant to peck at? When synthetic talk has no balance, when the intruder feels that the figures discussed have no life apart from their life in synthetic talk, then there is an urge to turn away: not

because of the influence of restraint (although that may be inde-
pendently at work) but because the reader comes to feel the reality
of the situation—that the cost of the transaction is being deducted
from his own shred of dignity, and not from some public figure's
ample store. On a television talk program it is the role of the host
to frame the synthetic talk. He must do two things: create a sense
of intrusion and then forgive the intruders. To do this effectively
he must obscure the flow of energy. He is honest when he implies
that his aim is to *grant access*. He lies when he implies that his aim
is to grant to a viewer access to a context. No context exists. There
has been no intrusion. No forgiveness is necessary. The true role
of the host is to grant, to a celebrated product, access to the viewer.
The intrusion is intrusion on the viewer. The host is on the pivot.
He does an important job. He pulls off the con. A particular view
of American history—the echo of *Life* magazine—is the host of
People.

Gossip is small, shameless history. It sets out to tell the trivial
about the great or about those connected to the great. It thrives
on awkwardness (that was the essential appeal of the Windsor
gossip: the endless awkwardness of it), because it assumes dignity
somewhere. "Somewhere else, you're getting a different story,"
gossip says, with a knowing look, "but this is what you wanted to
know." *People* does not assume that you're getting a different story
elsewhere. *People* does not assume dignity or powerful history, nor
does it assume that the figures it is writing about are actually very
important. *People* does not develop celebrities or announce them
or help them up. The figure on the cover is someone so well known
that that person can give a little sense of home. That the figure is
often bereft, himself, of a sense of home is ignored at first and then
is exploited if the exploitation promises to give us some comfort.
So Farrah is a story, and Farrah having a problem is a story, and

Farrah talking about her problem is a story. Approval or disapproval of Farrah is not a story; Farrah's talent or lack of talent is not a story; what Farrah has done or left undone is not a story. The only story is in the movement of Farrah's energy and the question of its magnitude. Is Farrah's energy so vast that it is undeniable? Have we given her so much that we can take comfort in the vastness of what we have given? The question has to do with something that is hidden, of course. But it's a different secret. Nothing to do with violation. Does Farrah do what we do? We know that she does. Farrah doesn't stand on her dignity. Not for a second. Nothing she does can give us a sense that she has violated herself. We don't wonder about that. We wonder if she *exists*. And if she knows that we wonder if she exists. And if it hurts when she feels that we wonder if she exists.

It was the habit of *Life* to offer different covers in different categories but always with this idea: that there was in the possession of the editors a sense of the variety of American life and American history to which they had agreed to give the reader access. Sometimes the cover showed a man of history, a general or a politician, and the sense conveyed was that this man was a man well known to the editors—especially, of course, to Henry Luce. In Luce publications, the world of eminent men of history had a particular flavor during the years immediately following the Second World War. In my mind, it is the flavor of Mr. Luce's house in Greenwich. The flavor of a small table, perhaps, on which there is a sterling cigarette box engraved with the name of an eminent man. Grand but *easy*. It was Mr. Luce's grace, during the years of his greatest influence in America, to bestow on his magazines, especially *Time* and *Life*, a sense of easy history. The reader felt elevated, in a way, and was encouraged to think, Yes, indeed, history was difficult, and, yes, problems were hard to solve, and, yes, stakes were very high, and, yes, decisions in this context must be very hard to make. But he was encouraged to find it all very simple, too. It was as though Mr. Luce had made an effort to show a person the most advanced mathematical system and then immediately made an effort to reassure the person that what he had seen was all based on the simple arithmetic he already knew.

Life also, very often, published covers that drew on the energy of a more accessible celebrity. It is instructive to compare these covers with covers of *People* issued on a corresponding day some years later. On January 8, 1979, *People*'s small cover lines were

Rock's Little Richard:
from sin to
salvation

How old is man!
Ask Richard Leakey

Sybil's shrink
diagnoses a rapist
with 10 personalities

Body Snatchers
prey, Brooke Adams

The large cover line was

IT'S SUPERMAN!

The photograph on the cover was of the actor Christopher Reeve in a Superman costume. The explanatory text under the photograph was:

And it's Chris Reeve
in the cape because
McQueen was too fat,
Stallone too Italian,
Redford too expensive
and Eastwood too busy

In addition, the cover gave the date and the price of the magazine (seventy-five cents), and it carried that ugly little black mark
that appears on magazines now as an aid to retailers.

Life of January 8, 1951, had a photograph of a young woman,
the date, the price (twenty cents), and the phrase "Circulation Over
5,200,000." The cover line, in small print under the photograph of
the young woman, was

STARLET JANICE RULE

When the two magazines are placed side by side, there are
obvious differences between them. The photograph on the cover
of *Life* is black-and-white. The photograph on the cover of *People*
is in color. *People* is 8¼ by 10¾ inches. *Life* is 10½ by 14 inches.
People's cover is filled with copy, mentioning many names. *Life*'s
cover mentions only one. The tone of *People*'s copy is friendly. The
tone of *Life*'s simple cover line is austere. But the important difference is, of course, that the name on the cover of *Life* is not a very
famous name. The graphic design of the two magazines emphasizes
the difference here, which is a difference in stress on what the foreground of the magazine is and what the background is. The issue
of *Life* for January 8, 1951, like all its issues at that period, had a
cover with a *frame*. There was a strong red band, 1½ inches wide,
at the bottom and, at upper left, a strong red rectangle, 2⅛ inches

by 4⅛ inches, enclosing the name *Life*, which was shown as strong white space against the red. This design made it clear that the magazine constituted a background against which, week by week, different foreground figures would appear. It also made it clear that this constant backgrouud was something of more weight than any particular foreground it might enclose. In the *Life* of January 8, 1951, there was no sense that Starlet Janice Rule outweighed the institution of *Life* in the American context. Rather, the reverse. There was a sense that the editors of *Life* had arrived at a certain authority over the American context and had decided to grant, for a week, the favor of their emphasis to a thing chosen, by them, almost at random. The favor might be granted to a girl identified (on the cover of the issue dated August 20, 1951) only as "400 Meter Swimming Champion," for instance, or to an unknown woman called "Beba" Spradling (on the cover of the issue dated April 2, 1951), who was on the cover because she had something to do with something that the editors of *Life* had decided to call the "South American Riviera."

The cover of *People*, by contrast, is without a frame. It is a foreground that suddenly appears—like a shout, or like teasing whispers building to a shout—and then vanishes. Its attempt is to create a foreground so powerful by being intimately connected to what one already loves that one picks up the magazine to find out the secret of one's own affections. Every cover of *People* says the same thing: "This is what you love. Who can you be?"

The cover of *People* dated April 2, 1979 (corresponding to "South American Riviera" and "'Beba' Spradling" in *Life*), read like this:

Kate Millet's battle for
women's rights in Iran

*Ronstadt's protegee
Nicolette Larson*

*Wall-to-wall celebs
at Phyllis George's
second marital flyer*

*Steve Allen's son in
a cult of God & Love*

The main cover line was

Who Will Cop the OSCAR?

The principal photograph on the cover was of Warren Beatty, with smaller photographs of Jon Voight and Robert De Niro. The three actors were shown as they had appeared in movie roles. Warren Beatty was in a sweatsuit, and Robert De Niro in jungle camouflage; Jon Voight was in a wheelchair.

The cover of *People* dated August 20, 1979 (corresponding to "400 Meter Swimming Champion" in *Life*), read like this:

WOODSTOCK REVISITED:
WHERE ARE THEY NOW?

*TV's giddiest guest,
Charles Nelson Reilly*

*The woman who checks
15,000 consumer items
for your safety*

*High seas violence
to save the whales*

The cover photograph was of Farrah Fawcett. The cover line was

WHY FARRAH SPLIT

The cover copy was

> "I am confused
> and frightened,"
> she says of her
> separation from
> Lee Majors,
> "but I'm
> determined
> to survive."

I talked to Richard Stolley, the managing editor of *People*, in his office, in the Time-Life Building, in New York.

"There is a difference in the kind of attention we give to the cover and the kind of attention we give to the rest of the magazine," he said. "We are a reportorial magazine, and we would like to keep it that way. When someone criticizes *People*, I ask, 'Do you read it?' There is a lot of good writing in this magazine, and a lot of good reporting. But we depend on single-copy sales—eighty-five percent of our circulation is in single-copy sales—and we are not a service magazine, like *TV Guide*, for instance, so the cover is crucial. We have developed criteria for cover material, and sometimes it works and sometimes it doesn't. First is timing. We put someone on the cover when certain outside forces are at work. A hit record. A hit movie. Best of all, a television special or a major news story. It is important that the attention that that person is getting not be exclusively the attention of *People.* It must be a coming together of forces. Recognizability, of course, is a factor. Attractiveness. And the cover should not be too much like last week's. Obviously, the forces we need do not always converge in exactly the right way. We do not have much control, really. In certain ways, the situation is maddeningly diffuse.

"For covers, the right moment is later rather than sooner, unless there is a real event going on. That's a difference from the way we worked on *Life,* for instance. The old way was 'Let's get it on the cover and be first.' Now you wait until the peak and maybe a little bit past it. Our *Amityville Horror* cover is an example of how we create covers. *The Amityville Horror* was the surprise hit movie of the summer. We didn't create the hit; in fact, from our point of view the movie had no redeeming value. The movie wasn't that good, and the story behind it seems to be a hoax, but it grossed forty million dollars in the first month and we decided we could take advantage of its popularity. Now, we'd already done a story on Margot Kidder, the star, so we didn't feel that it was appropriate to do that again. So we did this. We did a story on '*The Amityville Horror:* Hype, Hoax, and Heroine,' taking advantage of the fact that the movie was an incredible piece of flackery. Then we held it for a while. Each week, I'd look at the movie figures. I'd ask, 'Is it still building? Is it still growing?' Then, when I felt that the movie was beginning to collide with the new TV season, I ran the story. There was no point in holding it any longer, because the new TV season usually provides us with some covers.

"Now, the Farrah cover—'Why Farrah Split'—was the first Farrah cover we'd had in a while. We had felt that she was beginning to pale. We laid off, because she didn't seem to be working. People were sick of her. But then we heard that she was saying that she was trying to be a more liberated woman, and that added interest, and then when she left Majors that added enough interest to justify a cover. In a case like that, we have to have a face-to-face interview. If we can't get it, we will decline to do the story. A story like this is a kind of comeback story; it involves a certain expiation on her part. There is a certain technique here—for us and for the subject. The smarter celebrities can use a *People* interview to keep from slipping.

"In a way, we are very dependent on certain celebrities and on the movie studios and the networks—particularly the networks. There are only certain people we want, and they know it, and we know they know it. When you get beyond that small group into marginal people, you have problems of one kind or another. So we have to surrender a certain control at times. But we are able to determine the timing. We have fought for that. For instance, the network always wants us to do the story the week before the show, to build audience. We want to do it the week of the show, to build sales. We've won that one."

~ ~ ~

The Context of No-Context

The work of television is to establish false contexts and to chronicle the unraveling of existing contexts; finally, to establish the context of no-context and to chronicle it.

The Context of No-Context

Soon it will be achieved. The lie of television has been that there are contexts to which television will grant an access. Since lies last, usually, no more than one generation, television will re-form around the idea that television itself is a context to which television will grant an access.

The Context of No-Context

On cable: Flo Kennedy talks to Gary Indiana about Gary Indiana's new movie. In Gary Indiana's new movie, Gary Indiana performs a sexual act while an actress tap-dances on a driveway.

Channel 2: *Newsbreakers*.

Channel 2: Promotional Announcement. Made-for-television: A girl explores the world of porn when her sister is killed.

Cable: *Love for Lydia*. Alex drowns himself.

News: Iranians continue to hold Americans hostage. Bazargan government folds.

Cable: A man interviews his son about his sex life.

The Context of No-Context

A man interviews his twelve-year-old son about his sex life. Father and son agree that the most important issue is *communication*.

The Context of No-Context

A man interviews his twelve-year-old son about his sex life. In a state of weakness, the intimate grid imitates the mode of the grid of two hundred million, which it perceives as powerful. What could be more powerful than a talk between a father and a son? Many things. An *interview*, for instance, or something on videotape, or a discussion invoking the work of experts who have turned their attention to how a father might talk to a son. Pathetic, of course. It is as though, their little legs and feet gone into atrophy, people began, by the use of ingenious adapter kits, to fashion automobiles for use in the undertaking of chores around the house, all the while talking about "the need for transportation within the family."

The Context of No-Context

As television goes into panic, the truth of what it is will rise to the surface. *CBS and You.* It makes it clear. Nothing else exists. Just CBS and you. No city. No state. All those places where the series take place: *It's Boulder! It's Chicago! It's Indianapolis: Hoosiers!* All those places are *lies.* People will panic and want more in the way of company.

The Context of No-Context

Television has problems with its programming, because the frame of all programs on television is television—nothing else—but, to get through the day, frames other than the frame-of-just-television have to be used. Baby-play backgrounds. The West. A brave pioneer family pushes across the continent. Now This. But not all programs fight it. There is a superior candor in certain places. There has always been a candor in game shows and talk programs and daytime stories. Daytime stories are just television loneliness. Talk programs are just the television context of no-context. Game shows have come to admit that they refer only to themselves. ("For ten thousand dollars and a chance to join the one-hundred-thousand-dollar playoff, according to what you just said, what did you say?") Very rarely are contestants asked about the old history, the history before demographics became the New History. When this older, more distant world is invoked, it is made obvious that this world is mystifying and too difficult to be comfortable with. One game-show host asked a question about the First World War and then described the First World War as "certainly a military event of considerable importance." He was assuring his audience that the First World War *was popular in its own day.*

An Interest in History

People understand that certain things are "healthy" and certain other things are "not healthy." Recently, they have come to understand that certain things are "healthy" and certain other things are "decadent." To many people, a move to the country, the cultivation of a garden, the installation of a wood stove, by a man who had lived in the city and was driven nearly mad there, would seem "healthy." Similarly, to many people a stage show during which a group of young people damaged themselves and then destroyed a car would seem "not healthy," and possibly "decadent." But certainly it could be argued that the reverse was true—that the man who had moved to the country had abandoned any hope of having a share in the public culture of his time, while the young people who were damaging their flesh were involved in a legitimate attempt to form an aristocracy.

An Interest In History

What characterizes the culture of those generations born during and after the Second World War is, first of all, their dominance. Since the history of their time has been demographics, and not history, what they have been and what they have wanted has been the history of their time. Do people wonder why high prices are paid for Mickey Mouse watches? It is because of a hunger for history.

An Interest in History

So when popularity is the measure, things that were popular in the past can give a comfort. This works two ways. Very different. Not to be confused. But arising out of a single cause: the hunger for history. First, the purchase of objects from one's childhood. Second, the purchase of objects from someone else's adulthood. The first accounts for the Mickey Mouse watch. The second accounts for the rich young man who has had his duplex apartment arranged to resemble the public spaces of the Normandie. It is in an interest in *style* that an interest in hierarchy and history is first expressed among people trained to think of hierarchy and history as expressions of preference concerning trivial matters.

Adolescence

The culture, for reasons having to do with the working of the marketplace, did not make available any but the grimmest, most false-seeming adulthood. Childhood was provided. An amazing, various childhood, full of the most extraordinary material possibilities. That was it. Nothing more. Just childhood. An adolescence had to be improvised, and it was. That it *was* improvised—mostly out of rock-and-roll music—so astounded the people who pulled it off that they quite rightly considered it the important historical event of their times and have circled around it ever since.

Parody

Parody. Parody is very popular. Parody is an art form for children who have had imposed upon them a meaningless iconography or a trivial iconography or an iconography of excrement.

Defacement

When people grow older, they come to be responsible for what they know. If they then continue to refer to an iconography of excrement, they have to embrace excrement as worthy of their attention, and direct the enthusiasm of their fellows to excrement—not just to the discovery of the truth about excrement but to excrement. This is the movement from the excrement-childhood of television to a parody of television, to *Pink Flamingos* and *The Rocky Horror Picture Show*, or to the punk-art forms of excrement.

Defacement

Punk art is allied to what an extraordinary prisoner might do in his cell. Not ask for parole, for instance, or bone up on his case, but etch crazy feathery patterns into certain secret places. There's arrogance in it, and pride, too.

Defacement

Much advertising now lets the children in on the joke, and many American babies are coming to loathe the joke.

Defacement

Babies are babies, but they know when they are despised. But what if there is evidence, very powerful evidence, that the *way to comfort* is to join the body of the despised?

"You said ..."

"Our survey said ..."

"You said ..."

"Our survey said . . ."
"You said . . ."
"Our survey said . . ."
"You said . . ."
"Our survey said . . ."

No Authority

Questions. "What is your name?" is a question. "Do you know your name?" is a question. "How many times have I asked you a question?" is a question. "How many spots, physical spots, has your boss kissed on you?" is a question asked on television. It is possible to get it right. That is the trick of American con games. *You make it easy for people to think they've got it right.* All you have to do is give the answer the man gave. The man said, perhaps, "I've kissed eleven spots, physical spots, on her," and if the secretary guesses the number he said she wins a point. If the wife guesses the same number of spots, physical spots, that the man said, then she wins a point. They can get it right if they try. He has got it right by definition.

No Authority

The important moment in the history of television was the moment when a man named Richard Dawson, the "host" of a program called *Family Feud,* asked contestants to guess what a poll of a hundred people had guessed would be the height of the average American woman. Guess what they've guessed. Guess what they've guessed the *average* is.

"You said . . ."
"Our survey said . . ."

~ ~ ~

People

It is the superior candor of *People* to acknowledge that this is the process of history now. More ambitious magazines, or magazines descended from more ambitious magazines and continuing the names of more ambitious magazines—these magazines have to continue a dance in which they can attempt to obscure their loss of authority and confidence, their loss of the *active* principle. Magazines like *Esquire* and *Vogue* and *Time* and *Newsweek* have it as their function to dispense authority of one kind or another, but they know now that they have no authority apart from the demographic makeup of their audience. Consider it: all transactions involving authority involve an attempt to alleviate the sense of loneliness that is a condition of life. But when all partners in a transaction are passive, when the active principle consists only in describing the characteristics of the passive principle and playing on them, then no transaction has taken place, and the sense of isolation implicit in *no transaction* is increased, and everyone knows, deeply knows, that the attempted connection (which was coded in the syntax of success) has failed and left a dangerous residue, like an obstruction in the throat, which will make the next attempt much more difficult to complete, or even to fake.

The transactions of the American marketplace are very often criticized, but almost always what is addressed is the question of fairness. What if this were abandoned, perhaps only for a moment, and another question were asked: "Does this transaction add to my dignity or detract from it?" Or a still simpler question: "Does this transaction *exist*?" When people are involved in transactions that do not exist, it is not only their common sense that is put in danger but also their imagination. Indeed, imagination faces the larger danger, because in such a transaction common sense is ignored but the imagination is misused and debased.

Con

The con man does give you something. It is a sense of your own worthlessness. A good question to ask: "Does this event exist without me?" If the answer is no, leave. You are involved in a con game. When the con man tells you that he is about to present you with "a wide range of options," ask for one thing he will absolutely stand behind. Or beat him up. If he has some authority, you have a right to see what it is. If he is only describing the authority he senses in you, then do as you please.

The idea of choice is easily debased if one forgets that the aim is *to have chosen* successfully, not to be endlessly choosing.

1951: Life at the Beginning of the Age of Television

SOUTH AMERICAN RIVIERA
"BEBA" SPRADLING

What does "South American Riviera" mean? What does "'Beba' Spradling" mean? What does it mean, the way she smiles, shows a smile of teeth? What does it mean, what it says on the cover?

20 CENTS
APRIL 2, 1951

CIRCULATION OVER
5,200,000

The insouciance of the rich, first of all. Their juxtaposition of steel mills and baby talk. How little care they take! How little care they need to take! Self-enclosed but, in a way, accessible. Through their flaws or through their baby talk. All those steel mills turned into a smile. And baby talk. You don't know her. Never heard of her. Spradlings have lived and died and you never cared. But you know who she is. It's the Riviera. Not the old Riviera, the one we know, the one we know about and want to know more about—but only under certain circumstances. No. This is the *new* Riviera. The South American Riviera. There is a whole new Riviera. Better, possibly. It *exists*. But no one knew. But people know what a Riviera is, and what novelty is, and what a pretty girl is, and that rich people call each other baby names, because to one another they are just little babies, although they own steel mills and automobile factories and ranches running the width of the pampas. This is not quite history, because no one claims that anything in particular has happened this week (or any other) on the novel South American Riviera. But it makes use of a saddened, vaguely remembered sense of what history was. It evokes a place in history, and it announces, without excuse, a person who exists in a context, her own—the context of a South American Riviera—which continues on its own, without reference to its popularity among the mass of Americans.

It's not quite history. But it's almost reporting. There is, almost, a place known as the South American Riviera. There is, almost, a figure of importance called Beba Spradling. But not quite. And it's not quite reporting. Because they're quite interchangeable, a person has to notice—this South American Riviera, and this woman called Spradling—with a lot of other things. The message is presented with a certain authority, a little, self-assured baby voice of authority: "This is the South American Riviera. You really ought to know about the South American Riviera. This is Beba Spradling. You ought to know about Beba. Don't you want to know Beba? Know about Beba? We can help. She won't fight." But it's all a joke, because it's only a little general envy that's invoked, a small chip of envy and loneliness with Beba's face on it. No need for Beba. It could be Bobo. Sometimes it *is* Bobo. It could be Baba or Baby, or anyone. And it could be a new Riviera in South America or in any place at all with the right distance. It's not history, because nothing has happened, and it's not reporting, because it's no one from nowhere. The territory is loneliness and envy and the promise of access to a sense of ease. The truth, the history, is partly in twenty cents, partly in April 2, 1951. The principal truth is: Circulation Over 5,200,000.

Andrea Whips

At one moment early in the 1970s, at a time when Max's Kansas City had ceased to attract the people who had made its reputation but continued to attract other, newer people, because this reputation had been made, a thin girl named Andrea Feldman, who liked to be called Andrea Whips, used to put on something called *Show Time* in the back room. Andrea Whips was a minor Warhol girl at a bad time for minor Warhol girls, and *Show Time* had about it not just the flatness of diction associated with many Warhol girls but also *frenzy*. Once Andrea Whips had begun *Show Time*, it was hard to get her to stop. She used to climb up on a table or a banquette and repeat something over and over. "She'll be coming round the mountain when she comes" was something she repeated. As she chanted, she gave very specific readings to each of the words. At times, she would emphasize "coming"; at other times, "mountain." there was great purpose in her manner. Everyone in the room fed off it. If anyone had asked (as no one did) why she had chosen to stress "coming" during one recitation and "round" during the next, she would not have answered. If anyone had insisted on knowing, she would have answered with a drop-dead look or a scattered gesture. Andrea accompanied her chant with stylized movements. At one point, she would hike up her skirt; at another, perhaps as she was stressing a word—"coming" or "mountain"—she would tip her head to one side and allow that side of her body to relax. In these movements, too, she showed purpose. It was clear that to Andrea Whips at any one moment only one movement and no other, only one emphasis and no other, only one repeated act and no other had meaning. It was recognized in the back room of Max's that Andrea Whips was psychotic, but everyone knew she was onto something.

The Pointer Sisters: 1973

The Pointer Sisters were four black women—Ruth, Anita, Bonnie, and June—who wanted not to be poor, not to be unknown, not to live in Oakland, California. For a while, they were backup singers. Then, under the influence of their manager, David Rubinson, they began to sing songs in the style of the forties, in clothes in the style of the forties, in a manner that was Negro rather than black.

One night, they went by car out from San Francisco to a suburban place to see a performance by Josephine Baker, a black woman from St. Louis who wanted not to live in St. Louis, and who in the twenties learned how to embody one aspect of glamour and coquetry, and who, after that, had a sustained vogue in France. It was not the idea of the Pointer Sisters to see Miss Baker. A group of white fans had suggested it.

Down the street. Dark night. Certain flashing lights. "CONDOR . . . TOPLESS." Bonnie, looking pretty, said, "I just love to drive down this street. I can't help it. I just love those ladies." Bonnie had a nice fur coat, new. The Pointer Sisters drove right out of town. Things dispersed.

The theater was like a bunker—something in cement. The Pointer Sisters walked in. Inside, the theater was like a round room, with a small circular stage at the center. The room was not half full. People were scattered all around—gaps everywhere. Nothing tight. The Pointer Sisters walked past a door in the perimeter of the hall—a little door, a door with a curtain over it. Not a door at all, just something with a curtain. Behind the curtain, Josephine Baker prepared to make her entrance. "Why did they seat people at the back?" the voice of Josephine Baker asked from behind the curtain.

The Pointer Sisters walked down an aisle covered with a gray substance not much like carpeting—like something to keep the dust down, like something to cover cement. Soon after the Pointer Sisters were seated, the lights went down, and Josephine Baker *ran*— almost ran—to the stage: down the aisle, and over the gray substance, which must have been a pad for a proper rug that had been taken up. Josephine Baker wore a peach-colored costume, tight-fitting and studded with sequins. She looked just like a dream. Several things at once. A star, but that was just the start. Then a *lady*, but that was just the start. Then a lady who knew when not to be a lady, and how to please, and how to have a little moment of this and one of that. Not teasing—*flirting*. Does anyone know the difference? A tease is a con. You press a spot because you know that it can be pressed, and while the sucker is feeling the pleasure or the pain resulting from the pressure, you take something from him. "Do you have the money? Good. Good. She'll be right down. Wait here;

she'll be right here." And then, nothing. A flirt doesn't do that. A flirt does a dance within the context of giving pleasure. Referring to this, referring to that. And suddenly, following the references, you find a little surprise. Nothing enormous. Nothing like "Feed on me." Nothing like that. Something small with a bow on it. It's a pleasure. A surprise, and a *gift*.

Reaching the stage, Josephine Baker thrust up her hands in a gesture of exaltation. There was applause from patches of people around the room once they saw that applause was expected.

"Am I thin?" Josephine Baker asked.

Her coquetry dissipated in the round room. Nothing came back. It was a specific coquetry. Once, the line must have been "Am I pretty?" Her features, small and unusual, made it not quite arrogant to ask.

"And it took four or five hours to make myself more or less presentable," she said demurely.

"Why did she say that?" Bonnie Pointer asked.

"She *is* thin," Anita Pointer said.

Then Josephine Baker said, "I have an idea. It may be a bad one. You see, I'm being very impolite. I hate to be impolite, but in this great big round room I'm always turning my back on someone." Then, like a general, like someone who knew what it was to organize a raid on a trench, she gathered everyone in the sad, round theater into one section of the room and faced that section. Then she said, "Oh, ladies, you are so absolutely divine. You look like flowers out there." Then she held up a rose. She addressed the rose. "You're so stately and dignified," she said. She passed the rose to a man in the front row of the audience and told him to pass the rose around the theater. Her artifice drained into the room. Her artifice had depended on the effectiveness of certain small collisions— between things archetypically feminine, archetypically masculine, archetypically Negro, archetypically white. Essential to her performance was the idea of violation, and the idea that a violation could produce pleasure, and not damage.

In the round room, no reference had meaning. Josephine Baker referred to Paris as though it would mean a thing, and it didn't mean a thing. And Florence Mills, and this one and that one. She described a black actor but did not mention him by name. A man in the audience shouted, "Paul Robeson!"

"I didn't want to mention his name, because I thought you'd forgotten," Josephine Baker said.

Later, she said, "Thank you for coming and having the *courage* to stay."

Anita said, "What a sweet remark."

Later, Anita said, "You have to have more these days. People expect more. It's not enough just to come out and do a dance."

"Especially if you're too old," Bonnie said.

"She *is* thin," Anita said.

After about a year, there was a little dip in interest in the Pointer Sisters. Later, it got better. They left David Rubinson and forgot about the idea of the fabulous style of the forties, and it picked up. But for a while there was a slight dip. During this period, they were booked into the Club Harlem in Atlantic City. A big room. Crowded tables. A little idea of the previous vogue adhering to it. The vogue for glamour. That continues in certain black places, the vogue for glamour. In some ways, black people are more ruthless than white people about what they like and whom they like, and the power of fashion is well established among them. But certain vogues are of very long standing—the idea of glamour, for instance. The Club Harlem was one room in which what the Pointer Sisters did made no sense. It made no sense to refer to Negro modes as though Negro modes were new and fresh and amusing. It made no sense to refer to glamour as though glamour were an idea in need of help. It made no sense—that's all. Civilization went on at the Club Harlem in a more continuous way than it went on in the white world. The Club Harlem represented a real context. In retreat, but still in existence. The fact that the Pointer Sisters had been equipped with a little ad hoc context, a chimerical background for the foreground of their performance, did nothing to justify their performance from the point of view of the Club Harlem. The Pointer Sisters were unhappy. The juxtapositions that had supported them were gone. They were black women performing for black people in a black club, and no one got the point. "Why did David want us to take *a step backward?*" Bonnie asked.

About this time, I made friends with a black man named Donald. He was a criminal, more or less. He lived in what he called a penthouse. What it was was a room on top of a hotel that was a hotel for whores. In a way, it was a penthouse. It was at the top of the hotel, and there was a ladder up to the roof. In a way, it was just nothing at all. Sometimes Donald talked about his room as if it were a penthouse. Sometimes he talked about it as if it were just nothing at all. He always needed money. He got pieces of money from the whores, although he was not a pimp. On the one hand, he conned money out of them. On the other hand, he ran a lot of errands and so forth. He would give a whore a line and she would give him some money, so he was on top, but then she might ask him to go and get some cigarettes from the machine in the lobby. He said, "Who I admired when I was coming up were the white gangsters. In the movies. I'd go see any movie about white gangsters." He also said, "You see, the trouble is you can get *con-goofy*. You don't know where the con is anymore *in your own head*."

Drugs

And then this happened and that happened, and people changed drugs. Marijuana is the drug of breaking continuity; cocaine is the drug that makes a context for people interested in authority. On cocaine, people tell a different kind of story. And people are polite when they ask for it. It's not here? It's not in the next room? Is it, possibly, within fifty blocks? Could you, possibly, make the call? Would that be all right? Shall we go with you? Will you go alone? You're sure you won't mind? Naturally, there is money. That question. Naturally, we share in that. Suddenly, people so pretty, so well dressed, bring out their money, and it turns out that they have twenty dollars. Just that much. Or forty. Just that, and a few dollars for a cab home. What the mugger leaves you—money for a taxi home.

When people take cocaine, they tell stories that have in them an interest in context. They tell stories about a deal, for instance—how one thing is put together with another thing in a way that may result in a movie, or they tell stories about a problem, or a special scene. A thing looms all at once. It isn't there, and then it is there, complete. It makes sense. Like a problem. A problem makes sense. A disease. A disease can make sense. If it pulls things together into the disease, then it makes a kind of sense.

Sweet Babies

One of the sweet babies said, "He may have what kids have who have crib death. He was so laid back, this kid, that he stopped breathing. He was so laid back that they had to have a special belt, you know, like a sensor belt, all around him all the time, so that the parents could know."

One of the sweet babies said, "I had a virus and then I never had it again. When you have this, your sinuses expand and expand and expand and expand, until your whole face almost bursts. I had it, and when the nurse came in she looked just like an angel. Then I woke up and she didn't look beautiful at all."

One of the sweet babies said, "I went to an S&M club off Fifth Avenue. I couldn't believe it. It was *right off Fifth Avenue.*"

One of the sweet babies said, "I thought he was straight with me, until right now. Except, when I went over, I knew that this girl he was seeing had left for the weekend to spend the weekend with someone else; I knew that, and he knew that I knew, and he said that he *understood* that she had to go, and then he said that she *hated* to go, and he said that she was so worried about him that she *filled his icebox* with groceries to last the whole time she was gone. And then he went out to get cigarettes or something and I looked in the icebox and there was just nothing."

One of the sweet babies said, "When I was on the cover of *People,* they chose the worst picture. And then I couldn't read what they wrote. It was confusing. It was *about me,* but it was confusing."

World's Fair

When I was twenty years old, and again when I was twenty-one, I worked for the 1964–65 New York World's Fair. I did not just work *at* the New York World's Fair, I worked *for* the Fair, which is to say that I worked for Robert Moses. This was the one time in my life I have had any benefit from the network of connections which was supposed to be a feature of my upper-middle-class education. Because I needed a job, I talked to a friend whose father was the mayor of the city, and he talked to his father, and his father mentioned me to someone at the Fair Corporation, and I was given a job as Guide in the Office of the Chief of Protocol at the Fair Corporation, for seventy-five dollars a week.

We had several different kinds of writing paper. Writing paper was a feature of the Fair Corporation. The standard writing paper was so filled with embossed information that it resembled a puzzle. The name of the Corporation, of course. And Mr. Moses' name, of course. And then the name of the division to which the writing paper particularly belonged, and then, perhaps, the name of the person to whom the writing paper belonged. And the word "Unisphere," of course—for the vaguely atomic-looking construction that was the symbol of the Fair—and then a little ® by the word, and a picture of the Unisphere with another ® beside it, and, at the bottom of the page, this sentence, always: "UNISPHERE® presented by United States Steel." In the years since the Fair, I have often had my pleasure spoiled by a sense of the contract behind the event. I was less easily offended then, but I did dislike the Unisphere writing paper and preferred to use another sort we had, which said merely, "Office of the Chief of Protocol."

It did not bother me, nor did it bother anyone in our office, I think, that people sometimes confused our office with the Office of the Chief of Protocol in Washington. There was even a sense that we had a claim to a superior dignity. Certainly our standards were very high. We routinely had telephone calls *from* Washington, and we were instructed to say that we arranged Protocol Visits for "Cabinet level and above" only. We referred congressmen and senators to the United States Pavilion, which we regarded as an inferior institution, rather like a consulate. When a daughter of President Johnson came to the Fair, we handled the visit, but otherwise we saw very little of the government in Washington. We did see a number of governors, but this was because governors attended

State Day—promotional events arranged by the Corporation to honor states that had agreed to build pavilions. There was a State Day nearly every day, and it was a low-priority event as far as we were concerned, and assignment to State Days was not sought after by the Guides. In fact, we treated state delegations rather shabbily, although we were rarely overtly rude. They were met at the gate, greeted by one of the Assistant Chiefs of Protocol, and then taken out "on the site" by a Guide or two Guides. I do not remember that any member of any state delegation was ever taken to meet Mr. Moses.

We all came to know very quickly not just the hierarchy of possible visitors but also the hierarchy of pavilions. Planning a Protocol Visit thus became a question of matching the level of the visitor with the level of the pavilion. We were very good at this. In arranging State Days, for instance, we had several conflicting imperatives to keep in mind at once, and we weighed them all. The first of these imperatives was our own lack of interest in arranging these visits and a deep dread of being trapped at a meal by a state official who had the mistaken idea that we would want to sample the hospitality of his state. The second was the fact that a State Day delegation was usually very large, and therefore many of the most desirable pavilions would be reluctant to take it. Third, we knew that the visitors could be fooled *just so long,* and would insist on seeing one or two of the most popular exhibits.

We developed a little rhythm and a clever sense of misrepresentation: what could be represented as a good time, what could be represented as an obligation, what could be represented as special treatment, what could be represented as a sense of home. We started with a real treat. Most state delegations were given a *Glide-a-ride* in which to make their visits. A Glide-a-ride was a little motorized people-mover built by the Greyhound Corporation. Then we took them to *Illinois*. The Illinois Pavilion had several advantages. It was a state pavilion (the only state pavilion one could plausibly visit), so the issue of courtesy could be introduced—one state paying a visit to another state. It featured one of the Walt Disney automatons that were the hit of the Fair. And it was just inside the gate. The best part was, it was so boring and stupid that it was never, never crowded and the Protocol Contact at the Pavilion Guest Relations Office could be counted on to take any number any time.

It wasn't short, the show at the Illinois Pavilion. You could put the state delegation in and have half an hour to yourself. What it saw, the state delegation, while it was in was something almost sadistic in its absurdity. The Illinois people had paid the Walt Disney organization to contrive an automaton to resemble Abraham Lincoln. It was a somber automaton. The automatons at the General Electric Pavilion gestured and smiled and moved and did this and did that just the way a certain sort of person would, but the Lincoln automaton was less ambitious. He sat there, just the way he does at his great memorial in Washington—in that pose—and then he stood up, and talked and talked, putting forward a pastiche of his great words, and then, at a certain moment, he moved a finger of his right hand in a kind of twitch. Then, at the end, at a time when people in the audience were beginning to retch with boredom, he sat down. The pastiche he was speaking began to take on the form of the Cooper Union address, and he sat down. The sky behind him began to go blood-red. "The Battle Hymn of the Republic" began to play, and the sky resolved itself into an American flag, and he sat down. It was not so impressive, his sitting down, as it was when he *stood up*. It was the important moment of the show when he stood up. He did it in two movements. He pushed himself forward, head down, and propelled himself out of his chair. Then he raised the top half of his body. He stood. It was poignant that he *could* stand. After I saw this spectacle a few times, I realized that Lincoln was being portrayed *as a cripple.*

We often took state delegations to the Federal Pavilion after their visit to the Illinois Pavilion. This was a little dangerous, as the Federal Pavilion was very boring, but it was just across the way from the Illinois Pavilion and we were able to invoke the official aspect of the visit to make the boredom into a kind of duty. There were three parts to a Protocol Visit to the Federal Pavilion. The indispensable part was signing the book, which was the act of official courtesy. The second part was viewing the exhibits: something that could be done quickly—at a run, if necessary. The third part was taking the ride. The ride was an event that threw people deep into gloom. There were no amusing automatons, no singing dolls. Rather, a tall, narrow seat, something like a pew, moved slowly past a series of movie screens while an imbecile narration poured out from a speaker lodged in the pew at ear level. This narration had to do with American History, and it had a *booming* quality. The syntax was that of Walt Whitman, within a public-relations framework. *America* was made personal in a way that made her sound like a smug bully. "So you conquer a continent, etc." Emerging from this ride, one wanted never to hear another word about America or any event associated with America, and one wanted never to hear again any sentence cast in the historical present. Our office was careful never to send anyone important on this ride. Important guests came and signed the book and looked at the exhibits. Very important guests came and signed the book and left. It was embarrassing sometimes. A well-dressed official attached to the Federal Pavilion would be waiting with the book, and it was embarrassing to bring someone in and have an official of the pavilion waiting and then to leave right away when the pavilion had expected a longer visit. "Don't you want to take the ride?" the official would ask. He was a grown-up man with a career in the State Department. He was an adult working in the service of the most powerful government on earth, and his pavilion was not popular, and he knew it. After a while, we began to warn our Contact at the Federal Pavilion at the time we made the appointment. "Just the book, I'm afraid."

State delegations went on the ride, however, and by the time they emerged they were likely to be glum. They had been at the Fair for an hour and a half, and they had seen nothing, just nothing. Their special Protocol Treatment had involved them in two pavilions that no informed child would agree to visit. So then, as a treat, we took them to General Motors.

I can remember quite clearly what constituted a standard tour for a person of unquestioned importance: Ford, General Motors, the Vatican, Johnson Wax, and IBM in the morning; lunch at the Spanish Pavilion; General Electric and Du Pont in the afternoon. I can remember because I visited these pavilions more than fifty times each summer. I sometimes think that I saw more of them than any other living human being did. There were variations, of course. Johnson Wax and IBM might be in the afternoon and General Electric in the morning. Someone with children (or with a reputation for taking the Global View) might request the Pepsi-Cola Pavilion, where there were hundreds, or perhaps thousands, of tiny dolls singing "It's a Small World" in many, many languages, all at once, like polyglot peepers. Johnson Wax (the most exclusive pavilion) might decline even an important visitor if the timing was wrong, and we would have to suggest the film at the Protestant and Orthodox Pavilion. But generally an important visit consisted of Ford, General Motors, the Vatican, Johnson Wax, IBM, General Electric, Du Pont, and lunch at the Spanish Pavilion.

Lesser visitors, or delegations of unwieldy size, could not count on a tour of all these pavilions, however. Usually, we could arrange General Motors and Ford (not the VIP lounge, just the ride), but not always. The Guest Relations Departments of General Motors and Ford, while friendly, had been set up with the aim of offering hospitality to automobile dealers, and they were sometimes dubious about the importance of people we recommended to them. They were interested in all forms of standard energy, but exotic titles failed to impress them, and I remember, in particular, having difficulty in arranging the visit of His Holiness Mar Shimun, Patriarch of the East—the leader of a sect of Asian Christians. I was very aggressive, and I inflated His Holiness's importance as far as I dared. "He is the spiritual leader of two hundred million Christians," I said. The Contact at General Motors demurred. I abandoned the distanced tone we usually adopted. I said, "His Holiness really wants to visit General Motors. He's counting on it." Our Contact said nothing. I said, "You don't have to greet him. Just let him cut the line at the Futurama ride."

I knew what pavilions were important, and I knew what visitors were important. Pavilions that were important were pavilions that left no room for doubt. Pavilions that were totally persuasive. Pavilions that had solved every problem and left no room for doubt. Pavilions that had solved every problem and, from the surplus of what they had, had agreed to supply a sense of the-transaction-as-entertainment. Visitors who were important were important because they were important to Mr. Moses. Congressmen and senators were not particularly important to Mr. Moses, but they might come along on State Days, although those were more for governors. People from England and France were not important to Mr. Moses, because England and France had declined to build pavilions. In fact, people from England and France were the reverse of important to Mr. Moses.

Our building, the Administration Building, which was the seat of authority, was dreary in a certain way. Certain things were available—electric typewriters, for instance, and writing paper, and Touch-Tone phones. But not sunlight. Or very much space. One of the things that were available was a very long hall. You came in the door. Into a little vestibule. In the vestibule (1964 season only), there was a special little instrument that counted down the days until the opening of the Verrazano-Narrows Bridge. Sometimes I came into the vestibule and just stood with this, as you would stand with a friend. It was busy, full of purpose. Then down the long hall. Off to the right was another hall, not quite so long. This led to the International Division, the division of the Fair Corporation which had failed to persuade the governments of France and Germany and Great Britain and the Soviet Union and Canada, for instance, to build pavilions. International was headed by Governor Charles Poletti, who had been Governor of New York State for a month in the early 1940s, after the retirement of Herbert Lehman. Governor Poletti was always called Governor Poletti. Walking farther down the long hall, you came to the Industrial Division on the left and the Office of the Chief of Protocol on the right, and then, at the end of the long hall, there was another hall off to the right, and at the end of that hall was the office of Mr. Moses.

I saw Mr. Moses twice during my time at the Fair. The first time, he called me to his office expressly to congratulate me on the completion of a project I had undertaken. I meant to be winning, and I was prepared to be talkative, but Mr. Moses said something almost immediately about Yale, which showed quite clearly that I had been summoned to his office to share a Yale moment. Mr. Moses was full of that Yale spirit, which spans generations and reduces to nothing the distance between the head of the Corporation and its most insignificant trainee, but since I had not been to

Yale and knew almost nothing about Yale, I was silent until I was allowed to leave.

The second time I saw him, I was in the company of President Park Chung Hee, of South Korea. It is important to understand that Mr. Moses, having built the Fair, had no particular interest in what actually happened at the Fair, and no interest at all in people like President Park. Several layers of elaborately titled people were ranged around Mr. Moses to deal with people like President Park. There were elaborately titled people in the Office of the Chief of Protocol and in the International Division. In cases requiring special attention, Thomas J. Deegan, Jr., the chairman of our Executive Committee, was usually prepared to be helpful. But, unfortunately, President Park, in his long study of the modes of American power, had learned just who Mr. Moses was, and he was very certain not only that he was going to meet Mr. Moses but that he was going to have lunch with him. Now, Mr. Moses did sometimes have lunch, but it was not a usual circumstance, and it was very rare that he had lunch with someone who was not a friend or a member of his family or a member of the Class of 1909 at Yale. The moment was a difficult one. I left President Park at the little place where the long hall crossed the hall to Mr. Moses' office, and passed the desk of his secretary, Hazel Tappen, who had been with him through the twenties and thirties and forties and fifties and the parkway system and the Triborough Bridge and the Long Island Expressway and the building of the Fair and the building of the Verrazano-Narrows Bridge, and I went into the private office of Mr. Moses and told Mr. Moses that President Park was expecting to have lunch with him.

"What?" Mr. Moses said.

I explained.

"Deegan will do it," Mr. Moses said.

I explained that President Park had met Mr. Deegan but was not content.

"Deegan's the chairman," Mr. Moses said.

I explained that President Park knew that he, Robert Moses, had built the Fair. There was a moment's silence. Mr. Moses was reputed to soften under the influence of the verb "to build" in any of its forms. I asked Mr. Moses if he would go to lunch with President Park at the Spanish Pavilion.

Mr. Moses thought for a moment more and then said, "No. Medal only."

I then went out and brought President Park into Mr. Moses' office.

Mr. Moses rose slightly, then sat back down and gazed rather sweetly at President Park. "So what do you like about the Fair?" Mr. Moses asked.

"President Park is just about to go out on the site now," I said.

"Well, be sure you write and tell me what you liked," Mr. Moses said cheerfully. Then he rummaged in his desk and found one of the rather cheap medals we sometimes gave to visitors, and almost shoved it at President Park. Then, very soon, President Park left, and I followed. Just before I left, Mr. Moses said in a loud voice to me, "Don't worry. It's not a very important pavilion." I spent the rest of the day with President Park and five Korean plainclothes security men. At the Korean Pavilion, President Park gave *me* a medal even smaller and cheaper than the one we gave him. It read, "Distinguished Visitor, Pavilion of Korea."

Out on the site: So many different forms of transportation. A bus around the Meridian Road, just like a real bus. The little Glide-a-rides, and the little Escorters. Just like a private pram, the Escorter was. In our office, we sometimes had other things—special things —in the way of transportation. Cushman Cars, for one thing. Little electric golf carts. Not always. But sometimes. I had a friend, a woman in the Industrial Division, who had access to Cushman Cars. Sometimes she took me out on the site. She staged *raids* and took me along. It was the successful division, Industrial. Something more like the big time. Something less like Estoril. There wasn't a single exotic title in Industrial. They didn't have a governor or an ambassador or a princess. Just people who knew how to get from A to B. The thing about the people in Industrial was that they were going to have *jobs* after the Fair closed. And they had *standards*. Some things didn't meet their standards, and they *raided* those things.

My friend took me out in a Cushman Car. We went to raid the Hall of Education. So embarrassing, the Hall of Education. It wasn't exactly a Hall of Education. It was a Hall of a number of things. There was the *Daily News* Public Opinion Poll, and that was educational, and there was a place where you could sign up for the *Encyclopædia Britannica,* and that was educational, but some other things were less educational. We went into the Hall of Education. The Hall of Education was a sort of box. It was a box that had been meant to be divided into smaller boxes and then divided again. It had been meant to be kind of a maze. And it was a maze, but only for a while. After a while, the maze gave way to an empty space like a dirty clearing. For a while, there were cheerful exhibits, and then, all at once, there was just nothing. I came with my friend into the empty space. Someone had set up a little stage there; it was empty, like the space. My friend and I looked at it. She had heard about the stage. It was *illegal.* It was not in the contract of the speculators who had erected the Hall of Education that they should allow a sorry little stage. Then two people came in. There was a woman of middle age and a child—a boy. They were in costume. The woman looked at my friend in something like a panic.

My friend told me about the Garden of Meditation: "It was the World of Food Pavilion. Elsie the Cow was its big attraction. It was speculation, of course, but it looked all right, with the commitment from Borden. But it wasn't all right. Construction had started, but it wasn't all right. The money wasn't there, the commitments weren't there—just Borden. The building was about to go up, and suddenly it was very, very wrong. It was just before Opening Day, and it was very, very wrong. We went to Mr. Moses. He had everything out in twenty-four hours. Demolished. Out. It became the Garden of Meditation. There wasn't time for trees, I'm afraid—just grass. We moved Elsie to Better Living."

In some ways, the Fair was the loneliest place in the world. Usually, around the Court of the Universe it was crowded, but sometimes even there you could sense an empty space. There was a solid line of pavilions, naturally, but some pavilions were very lonely.

The Tower of Light. The Tower of Light was very lonely. Hardly anyone ever went there. It was such a good *location*. Near the Court of the Universe, the very heart of things. Near General Electric, which was so popular, and not far from Pepsi-Cola, which was so popular, and near Clairol, the Clairol Pavilion, where women lined up for hours at a time to get advice on their hair—the color of their hair, how their hair should be arranged. It was a good location, but it was lonely. Once, on purpose, I arranged for a person I didn't like to go to the Tower of Light. I put him in the Tower of Light and went away. When I came back, he was *so glum*. I had a big smile. It was one of my most American moments: meeting someone who was glum because I had pretended to do him a favor and hadn't done him a favor at all.

My friend in Industrial had a daughter, a beautiful blond girl. She was the daughter of my friend and a man who had been married, at another time, to Gypsy Rose Lee. The daughter came to work at the Office of the Chief of Protocol. One day, she brought Andy Warhol to the Fair. He was very quiet. He came with people. This was at the time when he came with people and stayed quiet. The other people talked and talked, but he didn't say a word. The other people referred to him, though. Without him, they would have had to shut up. In some way, he gave them permission to speak.

Sometimes Andy Warhol said something. It was simple, what he said, but it was not a comfort. He was *so polite*, but it was not a comfort. He used simple words, words that honored the idea of simple agreement—"Oh, it's so big!" and "Oh yes!" and "Oh, he was so cute!"—but there was no comfort in the agreement. And sometimes the agreement turned a corner. "Oh, he was so cute! But all he was interested in was drugs."

Andy Warhol looked like a little god. It was so comforting the way he made everything uncomfortable. And the way the damage rose to the surface around him. The people around him had this in common, at first: a sense of sin. They knew what was damaged and what was whole. Andy Warhol knew, too. But sometimes he was coy. Sometimes he wouldn't tell. People around him wondered if they had got it right. People around him wondered if they should be more damaged or more whole. It was hard to tell.

Popular pavilions: Ford. You got in a car, a Ford car, and the car drove itself along a track. A voice came out of the radio. Then you saw the history of the world shown by Walt Disney automatons. It was not complete. The Future was shown as empty highway. Suddenly, there was just nothing. In the sky, there was a kind of glowing ribbon. Just that.

General Electric. First, there was a display of Atomic Energy. It was a demonstration in a room that looked like a planetarium. A man (or sometimes a woman) stood in a white coat with a microphone and described the experiment. Then, after a while, he (or she) pushed some buttons or moved some dials, and there was a loud noise and a vivid flash, and the experiment was presumed to have been completed. There was a board showing the number of "successful" and the number of "unsuccessful" experiments carried out. It was convincing. The number of "unsuccessful" experiments was very small. One day, a man in a white coat who was conducting the experiment had a heart attack or a stroke or a seizure of some kind. People stood around him. People summoned other people. Meanwhile, the experiment, and the voice describing the experiment, went on.

Du Pont. Actors and actresses put on a show that honored various Du Pont products. One product was Corfam. There was a song about Corfam. In 1964, the song began, "We're going to have shoes like we never had shoes before." In 1965, the song was a different song. Corfam failed.

World's Fair
People didn't like the Fair. People tried to like it, though. They agreed to like it. The Fair was hard to like, but they agreed to like it. Not to like it was the same thing as to break the agreement that was all that stood between them and being alone.

World's Fair
The message of many things in America is "Like this or die." It is a strain. Suddenly, the modes of death begin to be attractive.

World's Fair
Who we were, in the Office of the Chief of Protocol, was something I did not ask myself. It did occur to me at the time that we were not all Americans. It occurs to me now that we were all refugees. The man who bore the title Chief of Protocol was an unsalaried political appointee: the Honorable Richard C. Patterson, Jr., former Ambassador to Yugoslavia, Guatemala, and Switzerland—Uncle Dick to my friend the son of the mayor. Not only did he have no duties; he did not have an office. He was a genial and polite man, but it *was awkward* when, on the odd impulse, he decided to come to work. For a while, on these occasions, we adhered to the fiction that the little lounge where the Guides assembled was his office, and when he came we went into the cafeteria for as long as we could stand it. But Ambassador Patterson was too kind a man to allow this once he found that he was subjecting us to inconvenience, and he asked for a little screen to put around one of the desks in the room, so that he could have some privacy. But this was so embarrassing an idea that we never got him one.

113

Our real boss was a stylish and sweet-tempered man from the North Shore of Long Island. He was a graduate of Yale and the son of an old ally of Mr. Moses. He drank quite a bit in a way that was entirely attractive. He was very loyal to us and rather contemptuous of the Fair except for the Spanish Pavilion. Once, when the Guest Relations Department of the General Electric Pavilion complained about me, he wrote back a note that said simply, "George can do no wrong."

There were others. There was a woman from a Polish princely family, a man from a Pakistani princely family, a man who had formerly been with the State Department, and Guides with every sort of unimportant social and political connection. But the stars of our office, the two Officers who defined the purpose of our operation, were Major Selma Herbert, who had formerly been a Wac officer with Army Public Information, and Dr. Roberto de Mendoza, who had formerly been Cuban Ambassador to London under Batista, and who was one of the last gentlemen in the world. Major Herbert and Dr. Mendoza did not get along in the ordinary sense, but they complemented one another in a way that was impossible to ignore. Major Herbert had angles; Dr. Mendoza sloped. Major Herbert had one kind of urban voice; Dr. Mendoza had another. Major Herbert was practical down to the last detail; Dr. Mendoza was a little *superstitious*. Major Herbert wore open-toed shoes; Dr. Mendoza wore luxurious ties, which he claimed he had bought from an elevator boy who stole them. Major Herbert never mentioned the Army; Dr. Mendoza never mentioned Cuba. Major Herbert called Dr. Mendoza "Ro-beh-toe" in a way that eclipsed all other pronunciations of the name.

The most memorable day I spent at the Fair was spent with Major Herbert and Dr. Mendoza. Together, we made possible something called Conference of American Armies Day. Dozens of Latin-

American Army officers were there. The Chief of Staff of the Brazilian Army and the future military dictator of Argentina. And General Anastasio Somoza, the head of the Nicaraguan National Guard. We had them in a Glide-a-ride. It was a long visit. It was long. We took them everywhere. The day stretched on. Every visit seemed so long. They liked everything. They were friendly. Dr. Mendoza was very sweet to them. We all were. We took them to General Motors, where they went on the Futurama ride, and to Ford, where they rode in new Ford cars through the history of the world. They saw Johnson Wax—the famous and popular movie *To Be Alive*. They signed the book at the United States Pavilion. They stayed deep into the night. They looked just like little boys. They stayed and stayed. We grew tired, but we did our job well. We took them back to the gate near the Administration Building, and they got off the little Glide-a-ride and got into regular cars. Cars with drivers. Black limousines. They looked a little different then, but the friendly, tired feeling continued. What I remember is Dr. Mendoza and Major Herbert *leaning over* as each limousine came by with our new friends. Dr. Mendoza leaned over and waved. Major Herbert leaned over and waved and called "Goo-*bye!* Goo-*bye!*"

Because it was so late, I took a taxi back to the city with Dr. Mendoza. Usually, I declined to go with Dr. Mendoza, because he always insisted on paying, but it seemed right to go with him that night. Sometimes, I'm afraid, I turned Dr. Mendoza into a father. Sometimes, for instance, I said something in the way I used to say a thing to my father—to provoke a story. There were favorite stories I liked to hear Dr. Mendoza tell. His voice had all the time in the world and a gentleness that couldn't make distinctions. In some deep way, he wanted only to please.

"Ah, there's the Tower of Light," I said as we left the Fairgrounds.

"The Tower of Light," Dr. Mendoza said. "The Tower of Light. When I first came to the Fair, before the Fair was built, when it was only the idea of the Fair, we used to have meetings with Mr. Moses. They were very serious, those meetings. I have attended other meetings in my life, but none were so serious as those, I think. Mr. Moses had great hopes for the Tower of Light. It was going to be a 'cathedral of light.' They said that, over and over. That and 'from Boston to Washington.' It was to be a cathedral you could see from Boston to Washington—the beam of light. But it didn't work out. There must be some reason. You can't see it except in Queens."

What the Fair was: The Fair was so small. It was just tiny.

World's Fair

What was the Fair? It was the world of television but taken seriously. A serious tone of voice. That was what remained from the previous orthodoxy—the booming voice. At the Fair, one could see the world of television impersonating the world of history. It was the world of television, but they wouldn't let you in on the joke.

This was what it was like when the orthodoxy of false authority gave way to the orthodoxy of television childhood. What will it be like now when, the absence of authority noted, a *vogue* for authority passes through the orthodoxy of television childhood? What are *children* like who are asked to salute? Some pout and won't do it. Some grin and do it badly. Some do it surprisingly well.

What is so defeating is this everlasting *good-spiritedness*, the application of enthusiasm against loneliness. The expression of the force that seeks to go with the grain—actually to become the grain—is, everlastingly, a smile. But the smile is a lie, and it makes people glum. And the glumness then flows against the grain, being confident of its bit of truth: *that there is a lie in the smile*. In our time, nearly all art has been made from glumness and has had very little power, because it feeds on this tiny bit of truth: *that there is a lie in the smile*.

It's so little to feed on. That little bit of truth. Feed on it only and you go mad. Nourished by just that little truth, how can you have strength enough to resist your enemies? The smile, for instance?

How lonely the white men are. They are not the grain that goes with the grain, nor can they bring themselves to dye their hair green. They thought they would have both things: the flow of history, because they knew history; and the *edge*, because they had talent. But history belongs to children, and the edge belongs to adolescents, so they have neither. What they have is a kind of superior whining, and the one freedom they have been able to make use of is the freedom carved out by certain adolescents to make an aesthetic out of complaint. So this is what they inhabit now: a tiny space where they struggle toward a sense of history and a sense of edge by refining their whimpers. *Something happened. What went wrong? I want to tell you about my divorce.*

Literary men now routinely tell their readers about their divorces. In newspapers. In columns in newspapers. Special columns devoted to the personal papers of literary men. One literary man who reviews books wrote, in reviewing a study of Ruskin, that he had never read a book by Ruskin but that the study confirmed him in his belief that he didn't want to read a book by Ruskin. This man very often writes about his family life.

Is he a fool? No. Absolutely not. He is doing what is appropriate. He is following a sound instinct. Instinct is so important. You have to go with the gut feeling. The gut feeling is that nothing could matter less than Ruskin. The gut feeling is that there isn't any grid to support Ruskin. The two grids left are the grid of enormous success—the grid of two hundred million—and the tiny, tiny baby grid of you and me and baby and baby's problems and my problems and your problems and *can we keep even this little baby grid together?*

And comfort? What is comfort? It's *focus.* You bring this grid together with that grid, you get the images to overlap, and suddenly things have a bit of focus, as in a certain sort of 35-mm camera. What shall we bring together? The two grids. You and me and baby and baby's problem breathing and the grid of two hundred million. *It is such a comfort.* So it is a comfort when the literary man who knows no Ruskin tells us how it feels in his marriage when a friend brings home a pretty young girl. And it is a comfort when a comedienne whom we know, whom we love, whom we've known for years and years, whom we've loved for years and years, tells us that there has been a drug problem in her family. Suddenly, the grids merge. You and me and baby and drugs together on the grid of two hundred million. It's so intimate. It's like waking up with a friend. But just for a minute.

Diary

EXCERPT FROM A DIARY, 1975:

When I was very young—four years old, that is, and five—it was my habit in the late afternoon to stand at a window at the east end of the living room of my family's house, in Cos Cob, Connecticut, and wait for my father to come into my view. My father commuted on the New Haven Railroad in those days, and walked home from the station. When I spotted him, I waved. I usually saw him before he saw me, because my eyesight was much better than his. When he saw me, he waved back and walked (I believe) at a faster pace until he was at our door. Once inside, he put down the bundle of newspapers he carried under his arm (my father, a newspaperman, brought home all three evening newspapers and, often, one or two of the morning papers as well), and hugged my mother. Then he took his fedora hat off his head and put it on mine.

It was assumed that I would have a fedora hat of my own by the time I was twelve years old. My father had had his first fedora hat at the age of nine, but he said he recognized that the circumstances of his bringing up had been different from the circumstances of mine (it was his opinion that his mother, my grandmother, had been excessively strict in the matter of dress), and he would not insist on anything inappropriate or embarrassing. He said that probably it would not be necessary for me to wear kid gloves during the day, ever. But certainly, he said, at the end of boyhood, when as a young man I would go on the New Haven Railroad to New York City, it would be necessary for me to wear a fedora hat. I have, in fact, worn a fedora hat, but ironically. Irony has seeped into the felt of any fedora hat I have ever owned—not out of any wish of mine but out of necessity. A fedora hat worn by me without the necessary protective irony would eat through my head and kill me. I was born into the upper middle class in 1943, and one of the strange turns my life has taken is this: I was taught by my parents to believe that the traditional manners of the high bourgeoisie, properly acquired, would give me a certain dignity, which would protect me from embarrassment. It has turned out that I am able to do almost anything but act according to those modes—this because I deeply believe that those modes are suffused with an embarrassment so powerful that it can kill. It turns out that while I am at home in many strange places, I am not free even to visit the territory I was expected to inhabit effortlessly. To wear a fedora, I must first torture it out of shape so that it can be cleaned of the embarrassment in it.